TECHNOLOGY IS AWESOME!

D1710907

101 INCREDIBLE THINGS EVERY KID SHOULD KNOW

ALICE HARMAN

Iosco - Arenac District Library
East Tawas, Michigan

ARCTURUS

This edition published in 2019
by Arcturus Publishing Limited
26/27 Bickels Yard, 151–153 Bermondsey Street,
London SE1 3HA

Copyright © Arcturus Holdings Limited

All rights reserved. No part of this publication may be reproduced,
stored in a retrieval system, or transmitted, in any form or by
any means, electronic, mechanical, photocopying, recording or
otherwise, without prior written permission in accordance with the
provisions of the Copyright Act 1956 (as amended). Any person or
persons who do any unauthorised act in relation to this publication
may be liable to criminal prosecution and civil claims for damages.

Author: Alice Harman
Designer: Sarah Fountain

Picture credits: p2m and p65t: Library of Congress; p2r, p19t, p19b:
EKSO Bionics; p7b: US Air Force; p8: Gravity Industries; p9b: Gravity
Industries; p18: Lulu Kyriacou; p22l: ARAIG; p33t: Lorrie LeJeune/
MIT; p38: SpecialEffect; p39t: Fred Davison/Quadstick; p39b:
Microsoft; p47t: Imperial College London; p62: Cmglee; p65b: Ammar
shaker; p66: Stratolaunch; p71b: Steve Nicklas/NOAA Ship Collection;
p77t: U.S. Air Force/Volkmar Wentzel; p91b: © Ecocapsule Holding;
p99bl and p99br: mimica; p100 and p101: Studio Roosegaarde; p108
and p100: Natural Machines; p115b: ICON/New Story; p118l and
p119: John Romanishin, MIT CSAIL: PI Rus Distributed Robotics
Laboratory. All other images by Shutterstock.

ISBN: 978-1-78950-022-6
CH006566NT
Supplier 29, Date 0519, Print run 7964

Printed in China

SCIENCE TECHNOLOGY ENGINEERING MATHEMATICS

What is STEM?

STEM is a world-wide initiative that
aims to cultivate an interest in
Science, Technology, Engineering,
and Mathematics, in an effort
to promote these disciplines to
as wide a variety of students as
possible.

Introduction

TECHNOLOGY IS AMAZING!

We use technology all the time, but there are so many incredible new inventions that it's hard to keep up! This book will give you the lowdown on the very latest developments, and take you behind the scenes to reveal how technology really works.

What is the biggest plane ever built? Why might a tattoo be able to save your life? How can a computer read your mind? All of these questions and many more will be answered in the pages of this book, so read on and open your eyes to the mind-blowing world of technology!

FACT 1
LIFE-SAVING DRONES WHIZZ THROUGH THE AIR

Have you ever flown a toy drone? You've probably watched an impressive sweeping video taken by a camera drone, whether you know it or not. But drones can do a LOT more than this.

Help is on the way!

Blood drones

When someone is injured and has lost a lot of blood, getting fresh blood to them quickly for a transfusion can be a matter of life and death. Enter the drones. In areas of the countryside that are very far away from towns, or that don't have good roads for ambulances to speed along, drones may be able to step in and save people's lives.

FACT 2
There are drones specially designed to spot sharks and crocodiles in the water and raise the alarm.

Defibrillator drones

Drones can also be used for carrying defibrillator machines, which can save someone's life when they are having a heart attack. A defibrillator gives a high-energy electric shock through the chest, which can start people's hearts beating properly again. In an emergency like a heart attack, where every second counts, a drone may be able to reach someone more quickly than a human team using traditional vehicles.

Lifeguard drones

In 2018, a drone made a life-saving first when it rescued two teenage boys off the coast of Australia. The local lifeguards were still learning how to use the drone when the boys were spotted, and they immediately flew it out to drop a floating rescue pod. The drone reached the boys around three times more quickly than a traditional lifeguard mission, and it brought them safely back to shore.

Finder drones

Scientists at the University of Zurich in Switzerland are looking into how drones could use artificial intelligence to find lost hikers without needing human guidance at all. They hope that drones will be able to identify trails through the forest and use facial recognition technology to find the right people. Once they've found them, they will send the exact location through to human rescue teams.

I've found Helen.

Wait, how do you know my name?!

5

STEALTH PLANES ARE INVISIBLE TO RADAR

We have developed many forms of technology to get a clear picture of what's going on in our skies—but stealth planes keep evolving to escape all of them and fly "without being seen."

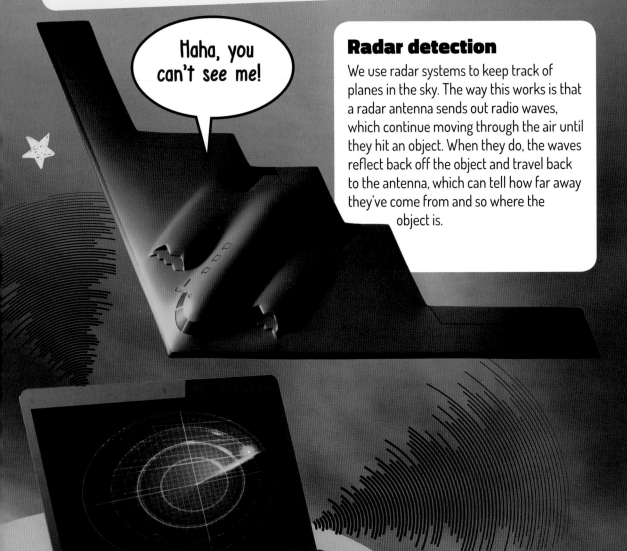

Haha, you can't see me!

Radar detection

We use radar systems to keep track of planes in the sky. The way this works is that a radar antenna sends out radio waves, which continue moving through the air until they hit an object. When they do, the waves reflect back off the object and travel back to the antenna, which can tell how far away they've come from and so where the object is.

Invisible design

The aim of stealth plane technology is to make them invisible to this radar system. Most planes are designed with a metal body and a rounded shape that reflects radar waves very well. A stealth plane can be covered with materials that absorb, rather than reflect, radar waves. It can also be designed with flat surfaces and sharp edges to reflect the radar waves away from the antenna.

Secret weapon

The first stealth plane was the Lockheed F-117 Nighthawk, which was developed by the United States Air Force and made its first flight in 1981. By 1983 it was fully operational, but it remained a secret weapon until it was revealed to the public in 1988. It gave the USA a huge advantage in the 1991 Gulf War against Iraq, and wasn't retired until 2008.

A F-117 Nighthawk stealth plane

Not really invisible

Stealth planes aren't actually invisible—if you stood in front of one on the ground, you would see it clear as day. But in the air they are more difficult to spot with the human eye than a traditionally designed plane. As technology to detect stealth planes gets smarter, so do the planes themselves, making themselves invisible to infrared, audio, and radio frequency as well as radar.

What do you mean my plane isn't really invisible? I thought I'd win this game of hide and seek for sure!

YOU CAN FLY WITH A JET-PROPELLED SUIT

Since ancient times humans have been obsessed with the idea of flight, and nowadays planes, helicopters, and paragliders can help us soar through the skies. But they haven't quite got the excitement of an actual flying suit ...

THE EARLIEST EXAMPLE OF MAN-MADE FLIGHT IS BELIEVED TO BE KITES, FIRST CREATED IN CHINA AROUND 2,500 YEARS AGO.

Wheeeeeee!!

World record

In 2017, English inventor Richard Browning set a brand-new world record for "Fastest speed in a body-controlled jet-engine powered suit". Catchy title! Browning made his record-breaking flight at the Guinness World Records Day in Reading, UK, reaching a top speed of 51.53 km/h (32.02 mph) on his third and final timed attempt over a distance of at least 100 m (328 feet).

Superhero technology

Browning has said that he was inspired by the hi-tech flying suit worn by the superhero Iron Man. The bodysuit is lightweight but strong, with gas turbines worn around the arms and on the back. It can travel up to 450 km/h (280 mph), although Browning hasn't tested it at anywhere near this speed yet!

Flying like a real superhero, that's the dream!

Fit to fly

Flying in the jetsuit demands a high level of control from the wearer, as there is no steering system—you just have to move your body in the direction you want the suit to move. Staying upright requires a high level of balance and core strength. Browning is an exceptionally fit person, and has worked on his core strength in order to pilot the jetsuit in a controlled way.

Jetsuits for everyone!

Browning can already fly in the jetsuit for over 12 minutes at a time, and he thinks that his invention could develop into a realistic transport option in the future. His company, Gravity Industries, has made and sold nine jetsuits—at £340,000 ($440,665) each. If you want one of your own, you better start saving up now!

9

FACT 5

ROBOTS CAN HELP THE HEROES HELPING YOU

There are lots of incredibly brave people in the world, doing jobs that put their lives in danger every day so that they can help others. What if robots could make their work safer?

Disaster zones

After a natural disaster, there are often many people who desperately need help, but the situation is also dangerous for those trying to help. Drones can fly into damaged buildings to search for survivors and send back information to human rescue teams about the situation inside. These drones use cameras and motion sensors to help them navigate on their own rather than rely entirely on remote control by humans.

DRONES HELP TO FIND EARTHQUAKE SURVIVORS FASTER THAN EVER—THIS SPEED IS CRUCIAL BECAUSE 90% OF PEOPLE FOUND WITHIN 30 MINUTES WILL LIVE.

Delivering aid

In areas devastated by violent conflict, it can be very difficult to get help to innocent people who are caught up in the middle of the fighting. Armed groups often set up blockades on roads and it can also be difficult for a crew to safely deliver an aid package by plane. Because drones are remotely controlled, the aid workers can stay in safer areas and send out drones carrying food, medicine, and other essential items.

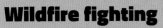

Wildfire fighting

Drones can be a fantastic tool for firefighters battling huge blazes—or they can stop them doing their job properly. It all depends on who is controlling the drone. An authorized drone feeds key information to firefighters, using infrared cameras to look through smoke from high above at how the fire is progressing. An unknown drone poses a safety risk to firefighting planes, meaning they can't fly overhead until it leaves the area.

Robot explorers

Exploring the depths of the oceans and outer space might seem like the kind of exciting jobs that we want to keep for humans, but it looks like robots might be better suited to them. Deep-sea divers face deadly dangers, ranging from pressure sickness to killer animals, and the health impact of space travel makes it risky for astronauts to travel long distances, so robots specially designed for these tasks are in development.

FACT 6

YOUR FACE COULD BE YOUR PASSPORT

Sprinting through the airport with your family, trying desperately to catch up with the flight that's about to leave without you, you suddenly freeze—you don't have your passport! Don't worry, though, this is the future ...

Biometric passports

Inside many passports today are electronic chips that contain information about the passport holder. This could be your fingerprints, your signature, and your retinal scans—pictures of a part of your eye. These biometric passports—sometimes called ePassports—also have information about your face taken from a digital photograph, such as the measurements between your facial features.

> Yes, it really is me.

FACT 7
Even identical twins have tiny differences that machines can use to tell them apart.

Next step

When you have a biometric passport and are passing through a border, you have to look into a camera while you scan your passport and the system checks your face against the information held in your passport's chip. Eventually, the idea is that the information about you will be held on the system and all you will have to do is look at the camera for it to check your identity.

Facial recognition

Smartphones are already using facial recognition technology so that instead of entering a password you can just look at the screen. Air travel is racing to keep up with people's expectations of a similarly simple, contactless process. The airline Qantas held a trial where passengers showed their passport once and staff took a scan of their faces. From that point on they didn't need to show a passport or boarding card—just their face!

Security risks

It's not just the convenience of digital passport technology that matters, though. Hundreds of thousands of passports are reported lost or stolen each year, which poses a security risk. It is believed that many more passports are not reported missing, and could be used by criminals and terrorists. Digitizing passports has its own security issues, though, as criminals can stage cyberattacks to try and hack into the systems and steal or change information.

FACT 8 AIRPORT SCANNERS COULD READ YOUR MIND

Terrorist attacks in airports and planes have meant a massive scaling-up of security over the past few decades. But the focus may soon move from checking your luggage and clothes to scanning your brain.

Airport security

Ugh, getting through airport security can take soooo long. Obviously it's to keep us all safe, and that's more important than a little (or a lot of) waiting around. But still, hauling your bags up for scanning and having to take off items of clothing just to put them back on again a minute later—technology must have a way of making it all a bit less of a chore, right?

This is taking forever. Where is the mind-reading scanner?!

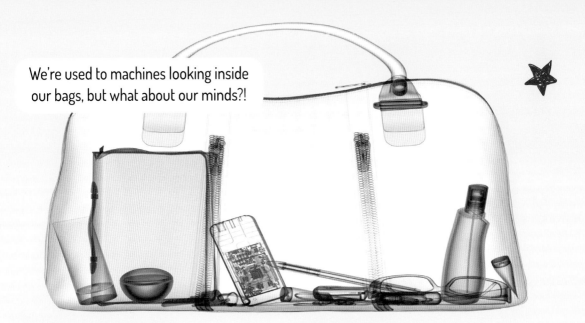

We're used to machines looking inside our bags, but what about our minds?!

Dangerous minds

Security experts are saying that the focus is shifting more and more toward trying to detect the unconscious signals that people give when they experience emotions and stress. For example, one system is designed to analyze a person's voice and tell whether they are relaxed or stressed. It has been successfully tested in a major international airport, where it was used to target drug traffickers and other criminals.

Screen test

In the future, you might not have to walk through metal-detecting gates or scan your bag because invisible technology could be constantly monitoring you. For example, an automatic check-in screen might flash up words and images linked to terrorist activities—maybe a photograph of a terrorist leader. These would disappear so quickly that you wouldn't realize you'd seen anything, but a positive facial expression could be picked up by the screen.

If floors could talk ...

In an airport of the future, even the ground you walk on could be spying on you ... One technology currently in development is a "smart carpet," with biometric sensors that pick up measurements such as a passenger's heart rate, which could suggest whether someone is unusually stressed. Researchers think this could be combined with tracking technology that follows a passenger's every step through the airport. Better safe than sorry, or just too creepy?!

OK, just hold still a second ...

SCANNING ...

15

ALL-TERRAIN WHEELCHAIRS OPEN UP THE WORLD

Without smooth roads and paths, it is a slow and tiring struggle to travel in a traditional wheelchair. In rural areas of developing countries, it can be almost impossible for wheelchair users to get around.

One in seven

Almost 1 in 7 people on Earth lives with a disability of some kind. More than 131 million people around the world need to use a wheelchair—that's more people than the populations of New York, London, New Delhi, Beijing, Tokyo, Mexico City, Lagos, Istanbul, Sydney, Los Angeles, Paris, Berlin, and Rome all put together.

Special wheels and no-rust materials make this wheelchair perfect for the beach!

Change of mindset

Even in big cities in developed countries, wheelchair users can often find that the design of public transport systems, buildings, and roads doesn't take their needs into account. Many places don't have step-free access, and finding accessible toilets can also be a challenge. The technology to make cities more inclusive for wheelchair users already exists—the focus needs to be on making sure that no one's different needs are forgotten or ignored.

Seriously?! How is this still happening?

Accessibility gap

In developed countries, where people are on average richer than in developing countries, more than 95% of people who need to use a wheelchair have access to one. In developing countries, that figure is less than 10%. In rural areas, having a wheelchair doesn't necessarily mean that you can have greater independence, as the roads and paths are often not suitable for wheelchairs at all.

Off road

If you have lots of money, there are electric-powered all-terrain wheelchairs that are the high-performance off-road jeeps of the wheelchair world! But there is also a new, low-cost manual all-terrain wheelchair called Safari Seat, which is made entirely from old bicycle parts. It is cleverly designed to be taken off-road over rough, uneven ground without getting stuck or broken, giving people more opportunities to do different jobs and travel safely alone.

This man in Zambia has cleverly adapted his wheelchair to make it easier to get around.

FACT 10
PARALYZED PEOPLE CAN COMPLETE MARATHONS

Robotic suits can help people walk again after becoming paralyzed—not just a short stroll, either, but farther than many people will ever walk in one go!

Marathon effort

In 2012, Claire Lomas made history by becoming the first person to complete the London Marathon in a bionic suit. She had been paralyzed from the chest down five years earlier in a catastrophic horse-riding accident, but with a robotic suit and a pair of crutches she managed to cross the finish line at the end of the 26-mile (42-km) course. Wow!

#claire

Claire Lomas creating a record in the 2012 Virgin London Marathon.

Pushing through

It took Claire Lomas 17 tiring days to finish the London Marathon, battling through intense exhaustion and pain to walk up to 2 miles (3.2 km) a day. Simon Kindleysides, who in 2018 became the first paralyzed man to walk the London Marathon, also pushed through a huge amount of physical pain to inspire others. Not only that—he said that the distance was actually farther than he had walked before he became paralyzed!

Super shells

The robotic suits are also described as exoskeletons—this is what we call a hard skeleton on the outside of the body, like a crab's shell. As the technology and design of these exoskeleton suits develops and improves, they are becoming lighter and easier to operate than ever before. The US Army has been developing a powered exoskeleton for non-disabled soldiers, so they can move faster, jump higher, and carry heavier loads.

The most important thing about exoskeleton suits is how they can help people walk again—but they also look pretty cool, right?!

It can take a little while to get used to walking in the suit, but it can open up all sorts of possibilities for people.

Getting closer

In the USA, it is believed that around 1 in 50 people live with some form of paralysis, but the number of people using robotic suits is still extremely low. The suits are very expensive, costing tens or even hundreds of thousands of dollars. However, as technology develops it often drops drastically in price, so it is hoped that in the near future it will become a realistic solution for many more people.

FACT 11 — TRAINS MAY BE ABOUT TO GET MUCH, MUCH FASTER

Imagine floating pods that shoot people across the country ten times faster than they could travel in a car. Science fiction? Maybe not. The idea is called hyperloop, and it may revolutionize travel.

What is hyperloop?

Hyperloop is a new form of overground transport that several companies are currently developing and testing. They have designed a train without wheels, which floats along inside a sealed tube on a cushion of air—like a puck on an air hockey table. Because the hyperloop doesn't touch the ground, there is no friction to slow it down and it can travel much faster than a traditional train—up to 1,220 km/h (760 mph).

FACT 12 Hyperloop is an open-source technology, meaning that its creators let anyone develop their idea.

Whooosh! I'm so speedy!

G-Force

Have you ever been hurled around on a rollercoaster and felt a swooping feeling in your stomach? That's what G-Force feels like. It is the pulling force of gravity or acceleration on the body, and too much of it can make you feel sick—or even black out, at very high levels. Because the hyperloop travels so fast, a slight curve in its path means passengers can feel very nauseous from the sideways G-Force.

The Shanghai maglev train

Difficult design

To avoid making even its most iron-stomached passengers feel very sick, people building a hyperloop system need to make sure that the tube it travels along is as straight as possible. The tube cannot be angled too much up or down, either, so the hyperloop must travel over fairly level ground. It also needs to be smooth inside, so that the train travels easily over the air cushion throughout the journey.

Maglev trains

Hyperloop is not the only "floating train" technology in existence. Maglev trains, which use very strong magnets to levitate trains above the track, are already in use in China and Japan. It is thought by many that hyperloop is a a cheaper and safer technology than maglev, so worth developing, but others disagree and think it will never work in reality.

FACT 13
A VIDEO GAME CAN TAKE OVER YOUR BODY

Video games look much more realistic than they used to, with new technology improving graphics and gameplay every year. But what if you could actually feel everything your character experienced in the game?

Gaming suit

You may already be familiar with consoles that vibrate in response to what happens in the game. But wearing a gaming suit, rather than holding a console in your hand, opens up a new world of sensory possibilities. You could feel the rain drumming on your shoulders, the aftershock of a blast ringing in your chest, or the rumble of a passing truck moving through your body.

Moving around

Gaming goggles and headsets available to buy now immerse players in the action—but without being able to move around freely, there's a limit to how real this can ever feel. New developments in virtual reality will let you walk and run during a game, with sensors that make you faster or slower in the game depending on how fast you're moving in real life.

Facial recognition

Another fun development for video games is using facial recognition technology to create playable characters that look like you and your friends. The company behind one of China's most popular video games is also testing out using facial recognition to check players' ages. If players are very young, the game could stop them playing for too long and becoming unhealthily obsessed.

Virtual school?

Virtual reality technology might make gaming more fun—but it could also liven up your lessons. Education experts believe that because many children learn better by doing something rather than being told it, using virtual reality could be really effective. Rather than learning about the ancient Egyptians, you could become one of them in virtual reality and explore the world around you.

FACT 14

SCIENTISTS WANT YOU TO JOIN IN

"**C**itizen Science" sounds a bit like the name of an educational superhero, but it's actually about using the joint power of all our brains to make incredible new advances in science that might not otherwise be possible.

Secret weapon

Hi-tech telescopes mean scientists can peer farther into space than ever before. But there's a lot out there to look at! The power of the internet means that by playing simple online games, such as spot-the-difference between two images, you can help scientists understand and analyze their data. You don't need to understand the secrets of the universe to help out—the scientists know what they're looking for and what it means, so they just need you to tell them what you see!

IF YOU'D LIKE TO HELP DISCOVER THE SECRETS OF THE PAST, THERE ARE ONLINE PROJECTS WHERE YOU CAN READ OLD LETTERS, DIARIES, AND OTHER TEXTS AND TYPE UP THE TEXT TO CREATE A DIGITAL COPY.

People power

Scientists, researchers, and other people trying to unlock the secrets of the universe have only so many hours in the day. It can take a huge amount of time to trawl through data, and although computers are getting smarter all the time there are still some projects for which they're not suitable. Luckily, there are a lot of people out there willing to lend a helping hand.

Wildlife surveys

Scientists trying to track populations of wild animals, and find out more about how they behave, can be in only so many places at once. As a citizen scientist, you can help them get a much more detailed picture by sending in information about the birds, bugs, and other animals you can see in your local area. You could also go online and look through photos taken by hidden cameras in nature reserves, tagging which animals appear.

Changing the world

By getting involved in a citizen science project, you could genuinely play a part in a scientific breakthrough. One particularly important project is helping researchers understand how our climate and environment is changing. In Belgium, around 20,000 people were given low-cost devices to measure air pollution in their area. The results showed dangerous levels of pollution, which varied between streets—these findings can be used to tackle local causes of pollution.

Describing what you see in each galaxy can help scientists solve the universe's greatest secrets!

THE INTERNET CAN TRAVEL THROUGH LIGHTBULBS

Wireless internet transformed the way we used computers, making it much quicker and easier to get online. It looks like the next step might be from Wi-Fi to "Li-Fi," using light to send data.

Woah! Nice job, lightbulbs ...

Wireless world

It's already hard to imagine a world without Wi-Fi, the wireless internet that means we don't have to physically plug in electronic devices to a phone line in order to get online. Wireless technology lets us move around freely without getting tangled up in wires.

Radio waves

The issue with Wi-Fi is that it uses radio waves, which are quite slow in sending data. A Wi-Fi router sends out radio waves in all directions and when a device detects the waves it connects to the internet. But these waves can also often get blocked by physical barriers, or affected by appliances such as a microwave—you may have noticed that the Wi-Fi is worse in some areas of your home.

Aarrrgh!

The frustration of slow Wi-Fi is real ... but may soon be a thing of the past.

Light speed

Scientists are developing a new, incredibly fast form of wireless internet that doesn't use radio waves at all. Instead, it uses light from LED (light-emitting diode) bulbs. A special LED bulb flickers at high speed to shoot out light that connects with your device, as a Wi-Fi router does with radio waves. You wouldn't notice this flickering, but it would be busy sending out data and keeping you online.

Faster and safer

Li-Fi can reach speeds of ten times faster than the latest Wi-Fi technology, and it isn't affected by appliances such as radios or microwaves. It is also much more secure than Wi-Fi because it works only if your device can detect the light being sent out by the lightbulb, meaning that you have to be in the same room or area as it. No one in the wider area can jump on your Li-Fi, as with Wi-Fi.

FACT 16

SMART CITIES ARE WATCHING YOU

Our cities have been watching us for years already, with thousands upon thousands of CCTV cameras in many world capitals. But what if the cameras could automatically pick you out of a crowd?

Being watched

The police can use these CCTV cameras to track dangerous criminals and to gather evidence in order to solve crimes, but not everyone believes that this is worth the loss of privacy. People also debate whether these cameras actually make places safer, and the evidence is unclear.

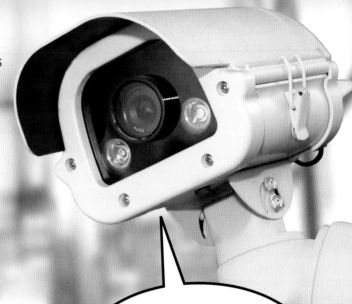

I never forget a face! And some people find that a bit creepy ...

Public trials

Facial recognition technology is improving all the time, and a number of police forces have carried out trials of cameras with automated facial recognition. These cameras were put up in public places and scanned the faces of everyone passing, automatically comparing them against photos of criminals stored in a database. The results were mixed, with many people wrongly identified as criminals.

Targeted ads

Imagine walking past an electronic billboard that greeted you by name and showed you a selection of products it thought you might like? We're used to targeted ads online, but facial recognition technology may mean that in the future ads in public places could also be personalized to fit what is known about you. There are already video adverts that change when they detect people looking at them—cool or creepy?!

Improving cities

There are also technologies that capture your movements when you're out and about in the city, without actually recording your face. Some cities have put in sensors that collect information on how many people or vehicles are moving through an area at certain times, so that they can plan and improve traffic and public transport systems.

Full speed ahead!

FACT 17

MORE PEOPLE OWN PHONES THAN TOOTHBRUSHES

Technology has changed the way we live our lives in many ways. For many people, smartphones have enabled them to access the internet for the first time.

5 billion phones

It is estimated that around 5 billion people across the world have a phone connection, while only around 4.2 billion people own a toothbrush. There are around 7.6 billion people in the world, so that means two-thirds of everyone on Earth now uses a phone.

Toilet systems

What's more, fewer people in the world have access to a flushing toilet than to a phone. Why is this the case, when we've had the technology for toilets for so much longer? Well, in order to have a flushing toilet you need a system of pipes to bring in the water and take away the waste. In some areas of developing countries, the government hasn't put these sorts of systems—known together as infrastructure—in place.

What do you mean, stop staring at screens all day? We're learning!

Internet access

For a long time, the lack of infrastructure in areas of developing countries stopped people from accessing technology. But the rise of smartphones means that people can make calls and get online with mobile internet, without needing a reliable system of phone cables. Phones that connect to satellites to get online can help get important messages out to isolated rural communities, keeping people safer and healthier and connected to what's going on in the rest of the country.

Online learning

The availability of mobile internet has the power to revolutionize education all over the world, but particularly in areas of developing countries. Children are using learning systems based on smartphones preloaded with apps, which enable them to study at home if there are issues with them being able to get to school.

YOUR COMPUTER COULD READ YOUR MIND

Voice recognition technology can be useful, but you don't always want to have to give a command out loud—maybe you're somewhere quiet, or it's an embarrassing request. But there are ways of speaking silently to a computer ...

Silent speech

Try "saying" this sentence silently to yourself, without actually making any noise. Done it? This is called "silent speech." You might not have done this since you were learning to read, when a teacher told you to say the words in your head instead of out loud, but you might want to try again now ...

Once upon a time ... oh wait, was that out loud? This is going to take some practice!

Reading signals

When you "silent speak" like you just did, you may not realize it but your brain sends electrical signals to your facial muscles to make silent micro-movements as if you are actually saying the words out loud. A device called AlterEgo has been designed to read these electrical signals from the surface of your skin, so it understands what you're "saying" without anyone else being able to hear it.

Brainy passwords

The AlterEgo device doesn't actually read your mind at all, it just seems to do so. But other technologies come a bit closer by measuring your brainwaves. The idea of brainwave passwords is that instead of asking for a series of letters or numbers, a computer shows a series of words on the screen and reads your unique brainwave response through a special headset. Research suggests around 94% accuracy in identifying the user correctly.

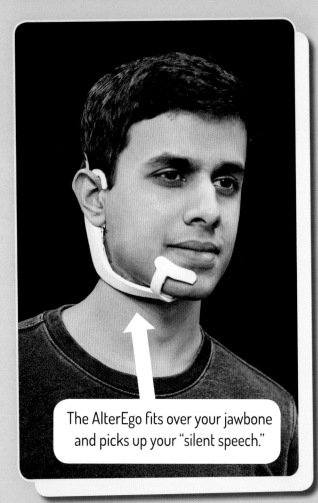

The AlterEgo fits over your jawbone and picks up your "silent speech."

Eye scanning

In the Azraq refugee camp in Jordan, thousands of Syrian refugees pay for their food at the supermarket with a scan of their eyes rather than with cash, a credit card, or even a smartphone. Iris recognition technology confirms the person's identity and takes the money straight out of the World Food Program's budget. The aim is to reduce costs, queuing times, and the possibility of corruption—money and resources not going where it should.

FACT 19 — OVER HALF THE WORLD NOW USES THE INTERNET

In 1995, 0.4% of the world's population used the internet—a total of 16 million people. By the end of 2017, this figure had grown to 54.4% of the world—over 4 billion.

FACT 20

China and India together have around a third of all internet users in the world.

Getting online

Access to technology varies around the world, and the same goes for the internet. Northern Europe has the highest percentage of people online—around 94%—and Central Africa has the lowest percentage at just 12%. Inernet access is improving, though, and every year the number of internet users in Africa jumps by around 20%.

Get off the internet, all of you, it's time for us to get some sleep!

Social media

What do we all do on the internet, though? Unsurprisingly, a lot of our time is spent on social media. There are around 3.2 billion social media users around the world, and this number is growing every year. The biggest jump in users is in Saudi Arabia, with India, Indonesia, and Ghana close behind. As technology improves and more people are able to get on social media, this global conversation is only going to get bigger!

FACT 21

Over 3.5 billion Google searches are made every day.

Websites

There are over 1.8 billion websites on the internet, but only around a third of them are actually active sites! Most of these sites are static pages that hardly or never change, and receive almost no visitors. Over 50% of web traffic is focused on fewer than 1 million websites, and within that a few hundred websites dominate the internet and attract a huge number of users every day.

Share, share, share!

The amount we share with each other online is pretty mind-boggling! Every day, more than 500 million tweets are put out on Twitter and more than 80 million photos are shared on Instagram. Around 235 billion emails are sent every day worldwide, but almost half of these are spam emails—that's annoying on a really massive scale!

35

AUTO-TRANSLATION LETS YOU SPEAK ANY LANGUAGE

Imagine if you could walk up to someone who doesn't speak a word of your language, talk at your normal speed and have them understand you perfectly. Well, soon you could do just that.

Magic headphones

You can already buy wireless earbud headphones that translate between languages in real time. The headphones pick up the language being spoken and immediately translate what is being said into your own language. Then, when you want to respond in the language the other person is speaking, you speak out loud in your own language and a translated version comes out of your phone speaker.

PAPUA NEW GUINEA HAS MORE LANGUAGES SPOKEN THAN ANY OTHER COUNTRY— AROUND 840!

Voice recognition

These headphones rely on voice recognition technology, which is becoming more and more advanced. But how does it work? Well, first a converter picks up the vibrations in the air which are created when you speak; then it translates them into digital information that a computer can understand. The system compares the sounds against a library of words and tries to work out what you're saying. It then translates your meaning into another language.

AROUND 200 MILLION PEOPLE USE GOOGLE TRANSLATE'S ONLINE AUTO-TRANSLATION TOOL EVERY MONTH.

Visual translation

Have you ever picked up a menu in a foreign country and had no idea what anything meant—and worried a bit that you might accidentally order something you don't like? Now visual translation technology is here to help! You can point a smartphone camera at the text you want to read, whether it's a road sign or a menu, and an app can translate it into your own language.

Lost in translation

Many people argue that automatic translation is still no substitute for learning another language. There are all sorts of interesting subtleties and cultural differences in languages, and perhaps a computerized conversation never feels quite like a natural one. But there are 6,500 languages in the world, and with more global communication and business than ever before, perhaps it's better than most people not understanding each other at all?

FACT 23

PEOPLE CAN PLAY MINECRAFT WITH THEIR EYES

Video games can be a lot of things—fun, addictive, frustrating, sociable, and an escape from reality. Surely this experience should be available to everyone, not just the non-disabled?

ONE SCHOOL IN SWEDEN INTRODUCED MINECRAFT CLASSES AT SCHOOL TO TEACH CHILDREN ABOUT CITY PLANNING AND ENVIRONMENTAL CONCERNS.

Eye tracking

Eye trackers—cameras that sense your eye movements—can be used with special software to play some video games. This opens up the world of gaming to people who may only have full physical control over their eyes. EyeMine is free software made by the gaming charity SpecialEffect, which enables people to play Minecraft with their eyes. It covers a range of ability levels, and is accurate enough for people to build, explore, attack, and chat freely.

Becky uses the EyeMine software to play Minecraft

38

Breath control

Some people are not able to use their arms and legs to play video games, maybe because they are paralyzed or because of another physical condition. A quadstick is a controller that senses the user's inward sips or outward puffs of breath, allowing for totally hands-free gameplay. There are also options for giving voice commands and using a push switch with your lip.

quadstick

Clever controls

Big video game companies are starting to take notice of the millions of people around the world who need to use adapted controllers. Microsoft will soon launch a specially designed Xbox controller, with two large buttons that players can press with their hands, elbows, or feet. It can be placed flat on the floor, a table, or the player's lap, and customized for different needs so that as many people as possible can use it.

Health gaming

Have you ever been told to turn off your video game and go outside to get some exercise? Well, it turns out that playing video games might actually be good for you after all! Health gaming is all about video games that are designed to improve players' physical ability. Players may need to move their hands in certain ways that help build up strength and control, and the fun element makes the discomfort easier to handle.

Xbox controller

YOU CAN TURN INVISIBLE TO MOSQUITOS

If you've ever had a mosquito bite, you know how itchy and annoying they can be. In some parts of the world, they can even be deadly. But maybe not for much longer ...

Invisibility patches

There may be a new high-tech weapon in the fight against mosquitos. Scientists have developed a patch, worn stuck on your skin, that gives out chemicals picked up by mosquitos. These chemicals confuse mosquitos' senses, making them think that there isn't anyone nearby for them to bite. At the moment, the patch works for only 48 hours at a time, but scientists are working hard to develop it further.

Where did he go?!

FACT 25

We are winning the fight against malaria—since 2010, the number of deaths from malaria has fallen by almost a third.

Tiny but deadly

The mosquito may not have a lion's impressive roar or a shark's ferocious teeth, but that doesn't stop it being the most deadly animal in the world. Mosquito bites are responsible for the deaths of more than one million people every year, mostly because of an illness called malaria, which some mosquitos carry. A child dies from malaria every 30 seconds.

Defending ourselves

There is no vaccination against malaria, and although there are medicines they are too expensive or unsuitable for many people in the world to use. In the past, some countries—such as the USA—have successfully used pesticides to reduce dangerous mosquito populations, but elsewhere this approach hasn't really worked.

FACT 26

Historians believe that Cleopatra, queen of ancient Egypt, slept under a mosquito net over 2,000 years ago.

Avoiding contact

The focus of many anti-malaria efforts is on avoiding people getting bitten by infected mosquitos in the first place. One of the main tactics used is covering people's beds with nets that have holes so small that mosquitos can't fit through them. These nets are treated with insecticides, chemicals that kill insects such as mosquitos. Obviously, these nets can't protect people for most of the day, so we need new, portable solutions—like invisibility patches.

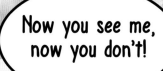

Now you see me, now you don't!

41

SCIENTISTS CAN PRINT YOU A NEW EAR

You can create all sorts of things with a 3D printer if you're lucky enough to have one at home. You might print toys, boxes, combs, whistles—the list goes on. But what about a human ear?

3D Printing

In the age of 3D printing, things that sound impossible are becoming a reality. A 3D printer can make an ear-shaped structure from a special plastic material, into which scientists inject stem cells taken from human fat. Our cells are usually specialized to do a particular job—for example, nerve cells, muscle cells, cartilage cells—but stem cells aren't fixed like this, so they can develop into all sorts of different cells.

THE INTERNATIONAL SPACE STATION, WHICH FLOATS AROUND EARTH WITH ASTRONAUTS ON BOARD, HAS ITS OWN 3D PRINTER!

Hey hey, I can hear you whispering about me!

Perfect match

As part of this new technology, scientists can use a 3D scanner to create a digital model on which to base the 3D-printed ear shape that will eventually be attached to the patient. If only one of the patient's ears needs reconstructing, the other can be scanned to use as a model. If not, a family member's ear can be scanned instead, to get as close a match as possible.

The earmouse

In 1997, the world was introduced to the earmouse—a mouse with what looked like a human ear growing on its back. In fact, the "ear" was a piece of cartilage (hard, gristly body tissue) that had been grown from cow cells inside a frame the shape and size of a human ear. This frame was made from a material that dissolves safely into the body over time, leaving the shaped cartilage.

Two ears are enough for me!

Building an ear

Charles Vacanti, who led the "earmouse" experiment, was inspired by another doctor who told him it was very difficult to create or recreate a natural-looking ear through plastic surgery. Doctors trying to do this still need to take a piece of cartilage from elsewhere in the patient's body—often the rib cage—and form it into an ear shape. It is tricky and takes a lot of skill and time.

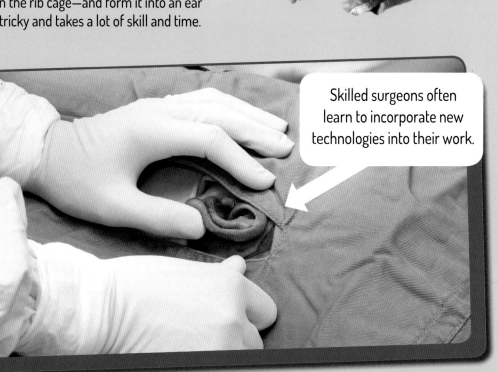

Skilled surgeons often learn to incorporate new technologies into their work.

FACT 28 YOUR MEDICINE CAN REMIND YOU TO TAKE IT

With everything going on in our busy lives, it can be easy to forget things—even really important things like medicine. But what if your medicine glowed and beeped to remind you?

Ok, ok, I'm doing it!

Take your medicine!

A huge amount of effort, time, and money goes into making medicines to treat all sorts of illnesses and conditions. But they can't work if people don't remember to take them! In the USA, up to half the time medicines aren't taken as they have been prescribed. It's a really serious issue because it leads to at least 100,000 people in the USA dying unnecessarily each year.

Glowing cap

People sometimes forget to take their medicine because they are busy or distracted, but for many their illness or old age can stop them remembering things well. To try to solve this problem, scientists have developed a "smart" bottle with a cap that glows brightly when it's time for you to take the medicine inside. Some designs also make noises, like an alarm clock, to get your attention.

Lifesaving reminders

These "smart," internet-connected bottles have sensors that can tell if you've missed a dose of medicine. If you have, the bottle sends out an alert to the company's central system, triggering an automated phone call, text message, or email to you. If you had a carer, the reminder would go to them, too, so they were aware of the situation.

Warning: This is not an alarm clock

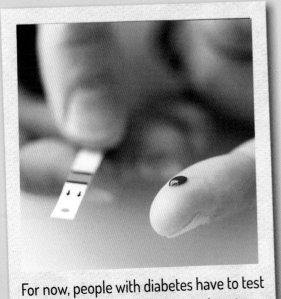

For now, people with diabetes have to test their blood with a finger prick test.

Fighting diabetes

New technology might also improve the lives of people with diabetes. People with diabetes need to regularly check their blood sugar levels by pricking their skin every few hours, which can be annoying and uncomfortable. But scientists are developing contact lenses and even tattoos that visibly change when they sense that the wearer's blood sugar is too high.

FACT 29
HI-TECH KNIVES FIND CANCER AS THEY CUT

A new weapon in the fight against cancer, the iKnife is a smart scalpel that can immediately tell whether the body tissue it's cutting into is healthy or needs to be removed.

Electrosurgery

The iKnife is based on a technology called electrosurgery, which was first developed in the 1920s and is commonly used today. In electrosurgery, doctors use special knives with an electrical current running through them. The electrified knife quickly heats the patient's body tissue, vaporizing it and reducing bleeding as the knife cuts. The smoke this creates is usually sucked away by a special system.

We're going to need a scalpel ... a SMART scalpel!

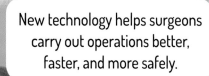

New technology helps surgeons carry out operations better, faster, and more safely.

46

Smoke samples

The inventor of the iKnife, Dr. Zoltan Takats, realized that the smoke given off when tissue is vaporized could contain important information. He created the iKnife by hooking up an electrosurgical knife to a piece of testing equipment called a mass spectrometer, which can pick out the different chemicals in a sample. Looking at which chemicals are in the vaporized tissue sample tells us all sorts of things about it, including whether or not it is healthy.

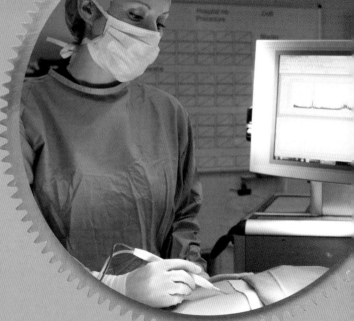

Tricky task

When a doctor is operating to remove cancerous tissue, it is very important not to leave any behind. This could allow the cancer to spread further through the body. It is difficult—sometimes impossible—for a surgeon to tell by sight whether tissue is healthy or cancerous, so they often need to send off tissue samples for tests or perform further surgeries to remove anything they missed.

On the spot

With the iKnife, the idea is that the doctor can know within three seconds when they have removed all the cancer—no waiting around for tests, no repeat operations. This makes things safer and saves time and money. It also means that the doctor doesn't remove healthy tissue unnecessarily. In tests, the iKnife was 100% accurate in identifying cancerous tissue, and it should also be able to analyze the blood supply and bacteria in body tissue.

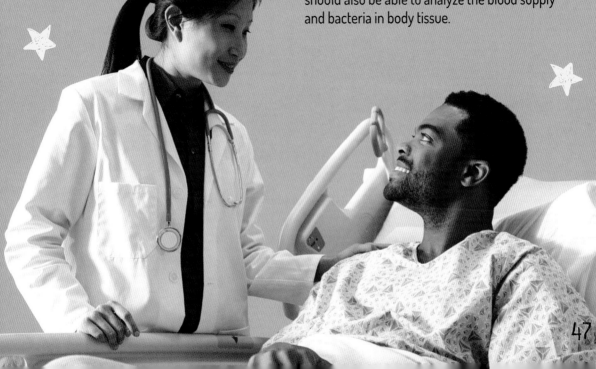

FACT 30

DOCTORS CAN TRAIN ON VIRTUAL REALITY BODIES

The human body is a very complex thing, so training to be a doctor takes years of hard work. It's a big leap from learning through books to working with people—virtual reality can help with that.

Learning to save lives

Some parts of training to be a doctor are quite like what you would do at school—reading books, watching videos, taking written tests on what you have learned. But doctors have to learn how to deal with the 3D reality of humans, which is a very different matter.

FACT 31

A 2002 study found that medical students who used virtual reality in their training performed the same operation faster and with far fewer errors than those who didn't use it.

Virtual learning

Virtual reality offers a way to learn independently and interactively. Students can try out new surgeries in a hands-on, practical way and can also be challenged to respond in real time to complications that might arise. Qualified doctors can also benefit from virtual reality, to keep up with new techniques and gain experience of medical issues they haven't had the chance to treat "in person" yet.

Woooah, this is unreal!

Breaking it down

Another benefit of computer-generated 3D models and virtual reality is that they can separate out different systems within the body, so students can learn in detail about each one—bones, muscles, organs, blood vessels, and so on—and gradually fit everything together. Different simulations can also be pre-programmed into the computer software, and students can get instant, detailed feedback on how they are doing.

Remote working

Surgeons are already successfully using virtual reality technology to be involved in operations when they are not actually in the room. They can watch an operation through a headset and appear in the room as an avatar to offer "in-person," live advice to the surgeons there. It means surgeons can learn from specialists in different hospitals—or even in entirely different countries.

FACT 32
YOUR TATTOO COULD SAVE YOUR LIFE

Tattoos are a very common sight in many countries today—in the USA, almost half of all adults has a tattoo. But biometric tattoos aren't just for decoration …

Check out my hi-tech tatt!

Body trackers

Many people today wear a watch or bracelet that keeps track of various aspects of their physical health—how fast their heart is beating, how far they've walked in a day, how well they're sleeping, and so on. Some scientists think that biometric tattoos, wearable technology that actually sits on your skin, might be the next step.

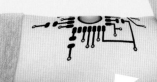

A biometric tattoo isn't just for show—it can give you highly accurate, real-time information about your body.

50

Not forever

A tattoo is usually permanent, drawn on the body by needles piercing your skin and injecting ink into the layer of your skin just under the surface. A biometric tattoo is simply stuck on your arm with a bit of warm water—like a temporary transfer tattoo. But as well as ink, a biometric tattoo contains electronic parts, which can include a tiny LED light. Scientists are working on developing a safe permanent biometric tattoo, but understandably there are concerns about trackers that you can't take off ...

Life saving

It is believed that biometric tattoos can give more accurate information than a watch or bracelet about things like your heartbeat, blood pressure, and body temperature. But they could also be able to detect when you are hurt or stressed, when a harmful material has entered your body, and when you might be breathing in poisons in the air! This may be particularly useful for soldiers in action facing serious risks.

Being tracked

People developing biometric tattoos have thought of many ways they could keep a close, hi-tech eye on your health, but how about helping someone else keep a close, hi-tech eye on you?! The technology could be used to track people individually—for example, to find a lost child in a crowd.

FACT 33

SOON WE MIGHT NEVER NEED ORGAN TRANSPLANTS

Some people with serious illnesses currently wait for years for a healthy new organ to replace their own. But soon we may be able to grow everyone new organs rather than taking them from another body.

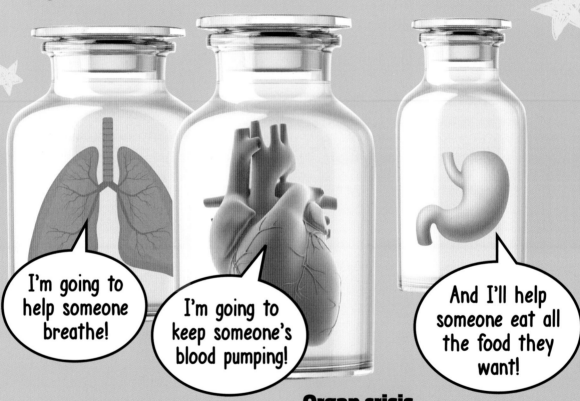

I'm going to help someone breathe!

I'm going to keep someone's blood pumping!

And I'll help someone eat all the food they want!

THE FIRST HUMAN ORGAN TRANSPLANTED FROM ONE HUMAN BODY INTO ANOTHER WAS A KIDNEY. THE OPERATION TOOK PLACE IN 1954, AND THE TECHNIQUE IS THOUGHT TO HAVE SAVED OVER 400,000 LIVES AROUND THE WORLD SINCE THAT TIME.

Organ crisis

More than a quarter of a million organ transplantations take place around the world each year. But many more people desperately need organs than ever receive one. Although many people choose to save lives by donating their organs when they die, it can be tricky to find a suitable match for transplantation for some people.

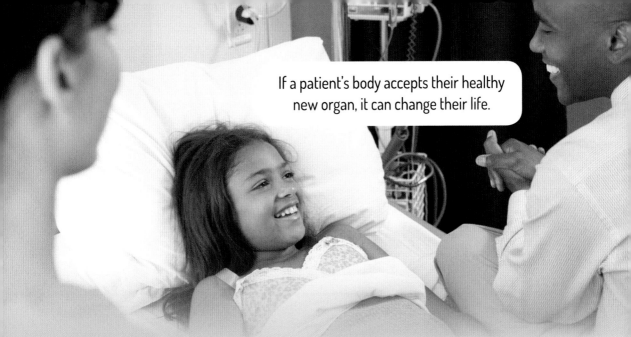

If a patient's body accepts their healthy new organ, it can change their life.

Avoiding rejection

Your immune system works hard to attack anything that it thinks might harm you, but sometimes this can be unhelpful. For instance, when a healthy organ is transplanted into someone's body, their immune system sometimes rejects and destroys it. But scientists have discovered that they can take healthy tissue from someone's own body and use it to make them a new organ, helping to avoid this risk of rejection.

Building organs

This organ-creating technology has been used to grow people new bladders in a laboratory and implant them successfully into their bodies. There are people now who have lived for years with these healthy lab-grown bladders working inside them! To build a new organ, cells from the patient's body are put in a liquid so they multiply, then poured into a model. Adding other cells and warmth helps the cells join together to form an organ.

FACT 34

Scientists are working on how to rebuild organs within the body, rather than having to operate on a patient. They were inspired by the way some lizards regrow their tails.

Future hopes

Some organs are trickier to create than others. Scientists have now grown kidneys in a laboratory which have been implanted in animals and successfully produced urine. They have also created a heart that beats on its own in the laboratory—though not inside a body quite yet. There is a possibility that in the future we will be able to inject lab-grown cells into the body to fight illnesses, too. For example, white blood cells help us fight disease, so growing these from our body tissue and injecting them back into our bodies could give us a boost to fight against serious illnesses such as cancer.

FACT 35
SCIENTISTS CAN REVERSE THE EFFECTS OF AGE IN CELLS

Some scientists believe that the first person to live to 1,000 years old has already been born. Could it be you? Would you want it to be?!

Reversing the effects of age

In the laboratory, scientists haven't just stopped human cells being affected by age—they've actually reversed it. But how do they know? Well, nearly every one of your cells has the same DNA, which contains information about your body, and at the end of each strand of DNA there are caps called telomeres. These telomeres get shorter as you age, and in their experiments the scientists managed to lengthen them again.

FACT 36
Scientists have found that injecting older mice with the blood of young mice appears to reverse the effects of age.

I'm 355 years old!

Ooh youngster, I'm 409!

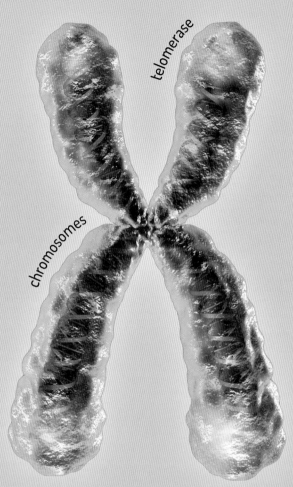

telomerase

chromosomes

Telomeres

Scientists delivered something called RNA to these cells, which pushed them to make a substance called telomerase that makes telomeres longer. The cells for this experiment were taken from children who have a rare condition called progeria that causes them to age far too quickly. Sadly most do not reach their twenties. Most of these children had telomeres as short as an average 69-year-old person.

Living forever

Successfully stopping the impact of age on individual cells, and then actually reversing it, doesn't mean that scientists will definitely be able to do this for entire human bodies—it's a lot more complicated! But if it is possible, it could mean an average lifetime in the future could be much, much longer than today. Combined with advances in other medical technologies, who knows what the limit might be!

Part man, part machine

The other possible way to live for far, far longer—perhaps forever—is to combine our human bodies with machine technology. Some scientists even believe that this may be the next step in human evolution. How do you feel about that?

THE LENGTH OF THE AVERAGE PERSON'S LIFE VARIES A LOT AROUND THE WORLD, BUT ON AVERAGE IT IS 74 YEARS FOR WOMEN AND 70 FOR MEN.

WE CAN WATCH BRAINS IN ACTION

Despite huge advances in modern medicine, the human brain is still a pretty mysterious thing. But scientists have found a new way to watch it work in real time and uncover more of its secrets than ever.

Hidden responses

When a person is in a coma, meaning that they are unconscious and can't be woken up but are still alive, they often don't visibly react to things like light, sound, or pain. But since the 1990s, doctors have been able to scan patients' brains while testing their responses, pinpointing which areas of the brain are activated. They have found that some patients are actually fully conscious, they just can't communicate.

YOUR BRAIN WORKS FASTER THAN THE WORLD'S MOST ADVANCED COMPUTER!

FACT 38 Detailed 3D scans of babies in the womb show them trying out different facial expressions.

Hey, stop reading my mind!

Wearable scanner

Traditional brain scanners are huge machines that require the patient to stay very still, which can be a big problem for babies and young children! But scientists in the UK have now invented a brain scanner that is worn on the head, which lets patients move around. This technology also means that scans can pick up which parts of the brain are responsible for different activities, such as drinking, nodding, and playing with a toy.

Scan my brain? Can't I just have fun with my toy in peace?!

Brain map

Improvements in technology mean our understanding of the brain's complex map of connections is getting better all the time. Scientists are creating maps of the brain that show details millions of times smaller than was previously possible. They use computers to combine different images, and shade in connecting parts of the brain to build up 3D maps. Brains of people with disorders can be compared with "healthy" brains to understand which connections might be causing problems.

3D printing

The brain is an incredibly complicated organ, and doctors have to be very precise when diagnosing and treating problems. Although 2D and 3D scans can help doctors trying to understand issues in the brain, a physical printed model may give an even clearer idea. Scientists have found that 3D-printed models of brain scans can more accurately show the shape and surface of damaged areas, helping them to understand different conditions and illnesses.

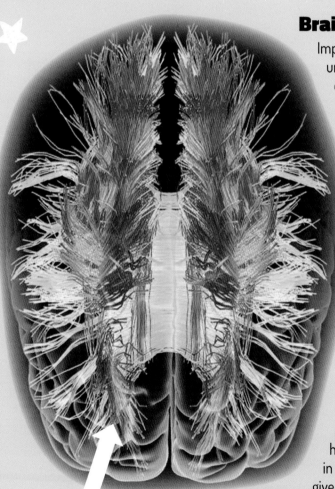

As brain scans get more hi-tech, we can see in more detail than ever before.

57

FACT 39

TEENY-TINY GOLD PARTICLES CAN SEARCH FOR CANCER

Scientists are learning more and more all the time about nanotechnology—science on a tiny scale that can have big effects. Gold nanoparticles are small enough to be sent through a person's bloodstream and can be used to detect changes in the body.

FACT 40

Richard Feynman, who first introduced the idea of nanotechnology in 1959, was known as a fun, eccentric character who loved playing the bongo drums.

What is nanotechnology?

Nanotechnology is all about studying and making changes to really teeny-tiny things, under 100 nanometers in size. To give you an idea of just how small we're talking, a single human hair is 80,000 nanometers across! Working with particles on this scale opens up whole new possibilities for treating patients.

Wheeee!

Here we come.

Time's up, cancer!

Gold nanoparticles can travel around your body through blood vessels.

Not just a pretty metal

We all know what gold is about, right? It's a yellow, easily shaped metal that we like to make into rings, necklaces and other shiny, pretty things. It's not very exciting in a chemical reaction, because it doesn't do much. Well, on a nanoscale it becomes much more interesting! A gold nanoparticle has more atoms on its surface than a bigger gold particle, making it react much more intensely with its surroundings.

Yes, yes, I'm gorgeous, but don't you know I save lives too?!

Gold soldiers

Scientists have added antibodies (disease-fighting human proteins) to gold nanoparticles and sent them into the body. The antibodies lock on to cancer cells, meaning that the gold nanoparticles cluster around the cancerous area. Scientists can then use a laser to blast the gold, destroying the cancer and leaving healthy cells intact.

Small scale, big bucks!

Nanotechnology isn't just used in ground-breaking medical research, though—it's big business! Companies developing the latest cosmetics, phones, and sports gear already use nanotechnology to customize materials to do exactly what they want them to do. For instance, nanoparticles in skin creams can carry powerful ingredients through the top layer of our skin to make a bigger difference deeper under the surface.

Scientists hard at work exploring the teeny-tiny world of nanotechnology.

FACT 41 DOCTORS CAN READ YOUR DNA

DNA is the material that contains all the information about how a living thing looks and functions. Scientists now understand how to read the information in DNA, and this discovery could help keep you healthy.

The human genome

DNA is made up of lots of smaller parts, called bases, which combine to make genes. Scientists think there are around 20,000 genes in the human genome, which is the complete set of instructions for how to make a human! Different people have slightly different genes, and these differences can mean we are more or less likely to develop certain conditions and diseases.

DNA helix

NEW TECHNOLOGIES COULD ENABLE US TO MAKE CHANGES TO A PERSON'S GENOME, TAKING OUT GENES THAT ARE LINKED TO SERIOUS DISEASES.

Learning to read

Until very recently, we couldn't read anyone's DNA at all. In 1990, a team of hundreds of scientists from all over the world began trying to work out the exact make-up of the human genome of a man and woman. Their aim was to complete this huge, ground-breaking discovery within 15 years—they managed it in 13. Um, over-achievers much?!

More mapping

The Human Genome Project cost around $2.7 billion in total. Nowadays, it takes around two days and $1,000 to map a person's genome, and the cost and time is likely to keep getting much faster and cheaper. This means that many more people can find out about their DNA and what it might mean for their health.

Doctors can get a DNA sample from someone simply by rubbing the inside of their cheek with a cotton swab.

Personalized medicine

Scientists predict that the easy availability of DNA mapping will mean a total change for medicine, with doctors prescribing individualized treatment for patients based on their DNA rather than a "one size fits all" approach. People can make choices based on what they know about their DNA—for instance, women who have a high genetic risk of breast cancer now sometimes choose to have surgery to remove their breast tissue.

DNA-mapping technology may take medicine up to the next level!

FACT 42 A CAR CAN TRAVEL FASTER THAN SOUND

The fastest speed ever achieved on land so far is an amazing 1,227.985 km/h (763.035 mph). Talk about life in the fast lane!

FACT 43 The ThrustSSC is more than 75 times faster than the first car ever driven, back in 1886.

Land speed record

The current world record for the fastest vehicle on land was set back in 1997, by a car called ThrustSSC. It went almost three times quicker than the fastest racing car ever recorded! It was the first time a car had ever broken the sound barrier, which means being so speedy that it actually overtook sound!

I'm unbeatable!

Check out how speedy we are up here!

Speed of sound

Sound travels in waves, and the speed at which these waves travel changes. For instance, sound travels faster on a warm day than a cold one, and faster through thin, cold mountain air than through air in areas that are roughly level with the sea. On a warm day in an area of land at sea level, sound travels at around 1,220 km/h (760 mph).

Sonic boom

When a car—or, more usually, a plane—breaks the sound barrier by moving faster than the speed of sound, boy do you know about it! It creates a sonic boom, which sounds like an explosion or a huge clap of thunder. You hear a mini sonic boom when someone cracks a whip— but imagine that being made by something as big as a car or a plane!

Even faster

It's been quite a while now since the land speed record was set, but the team behind a new car designed to go 1,610 km/h (1,000 mph) think they can break it. The Bloodhound SSC car is powered by a jet fighter engine and a number of rockets. It is still in the testing stage, but the aim is for it to cover 1.6 km (1 mile) in just over three and a half seconds!

When an aircraft travels through moist air at supersonic speeds, you can sometimes see a visible cloud of water droplets form around it.

FACT 44

OLD SKYSCRAPERS LOOK TINY TO US NOW

The world's first skyscraper was built in 1885 and was ten floors tall. The tallest completed building in the world, the Burj Khalifa, is more than 15 times higher than this first official skyscraper.

Building into the sky

At the time that it was built, the first skyscraper—the Home Insurance Building in Chicago, USA—was an unbelievably impressive and modern sight. Now it's completely normal for people to live in buildings that are much, much taller. Technology has helped us build so much higher that it feels like we're no longer scraping the sky—we're living in it.

Aah, you guys look so tiny from up here!

Show-off!

The Burj Khalifa towers above other skyscrapers in the city of Dubai.

FACT 45

Skyscrapers in London, UK, sometimes have funny nicknames that describe what they look like—you can spot the Gherkin, the Cheese Grater, and the Walkie-Talkie in the city skyline.

Home Insurance Building

The first skyscraper

The Home Insurance Building looked like an entirely brick building from the outside, but it included a steel frame to support the building's great weight. The building was knocked down in 1931, the same year that the iconic Empire State Building was completed in New York, USA. All these years later, the Empire State Building is probably still the world's most famous skyscraper.

Burj Khalifa

The Burj Khalifa in Dubai, United Arab Emirates, is the world's tallest building. It stands an impressive 828 m (2,716 ft), with over 160 floors. If all the pieces that make up the Burj Khalifa were laid end to end, they would stretch over a quarter of the way around the world!

Jeddah Tower

The Jeddah Tower is currently under construction in Jeddah, Saudi Arabia, and is set to steal Burj Khalifa's title of world's tallest building. Originally, the developers wanted the tower to be 1.6 km (1 mile) high— but soil testing in the area showed that the ground wasn't right to safely support that height. So now it's planned to be around 1 km (0.62 miles) high—still tall enough to break the record.

Watch out Burj Khalifa, I'm heading for the top spot!

Jeddah Tower under construction

65

THERE IS A PLANE 10 TENNIS COURTS WIDE

How roomy! Or is it? Actually it's the wings, rather than the entire body of the plane, that reach this incredible size. But the plane is so big it needs six engines to take off!

Double the fun

Stratolaunch is the largest plane ever built. It is so big that it needs two separate cockpits to control it, and it has 28 wheels for taking off and landing. But this giant of the skies isn't just made for carrying people to and fro across the world—it is designed to launch them into space.

FACT 47

The Lockheed Blackbird holds the record for the fastest plane in the world. It was a US military aircraft that reached a top speed of 3,529 km/h (2,193 mph) in 1976. It could outrun missiles!

Access to space

Stratolaunch is designed to carry one or more rockets underneath its wings. These rockets could carry objects such as satellites, making it quicker and easier to get them up into space and circling around Earth. The idea is to make rocket launches into space as easy and everyday as catching a plane to another country.

First flights

We've come a long way since the first plane flight in 1903, which was an incredibly impressive but very short and uncomfortable journey! You may have heard of the inventors of this plane—the Wright Brothers. Only 11 years later the first commercial flight—one with paying passengers—took place between the cities of St. Petersburg and Tampa in Florida, USA. Today, there are 37.5 million flights every year—that's more than one flight per second!

Wooah, it's a bit of a bumpy ride!

A Wright Brothers' plane flying in 1904.

Concorde in flight

Not so fast

The average cruising speed for a commercial plane today is around 925 km/h (575 mph). That's pretty fast, but planes can go a lot quicker. Concorde was a passenger plane that could travel at 2,179 km/h (1,354 mph)—over twice the speed of sound. It was retired in 2003, apparently because not enough people were willing to pay the high cost for a shorter flight.

I can't believe you stopped me flying. Look how fast I can go!

FACT 48

WE CAN SEE 13.2 BILLION YEARS INTO THE PAST

New technology enables scientists to see areas of space so far away that light takes 13.2 billion years to reach us from there. Looking at these areas is seeing into their ancient past.

The Hubble Telescope

The incredibly powerful Hubble Telescope can see deeper into outer space than we've ever been able to before. It circles around Earth, up beyond the clouds and gases of our planet's atmosphere, which gives it a much clearer view. It can see incredibly faint, far-away objects that even very powerful telescopes on Earth can't spot.

FACT 49

The Hubble telescope is powered by the Sun's energy.

Oh man, check out the view from up here!

Speeding light

Light travels incredibly quickly—if you could move at the speed of light, you could circle the Earth seven times in a single second. In one year, light can travel 9.5 trillion kilometres (5.9 trillion miles), which is like zooming around Earth 237 million times. Light is coming to us from places across the universe that are over 13 billion times this distance away—it's almost impossible to really imagine how far away it really is!

Long, long ago

The universe is around 13.7 billion years old, so being able to see an area as it looked 13.2 billion years ago means that we know how it looked in the early days of the universe. A lot can change between then and now, obviously. Some of the stars we see as they were billions of years ago may have run out of fuel and no longer exist.

Seeing into the past

When the light arrives from these far-off areas of space, it shows us what they looked like when the light left all that time ago. If aliens exist and can see far enough into space, they will see Earth as it looked in the past—for example, if light from Earth takes 65 million years to reach them, they will see our planet as it looked in the time of the dinosaurs.

Looking at all these ancient stars makes me feel so young, woohoo!

FACT 50
WE'VE FINALLY REACHED THE DEEPEST POINT ON EARTH

We're actually making better progress exploring outer space than we are with our own oceans. The lowest point on Earth, far under the sea, is as almost as weird and mysterious as deep space.

The Challenger Deep

It sounds like the name of a spacecraft, or maybe the title of a science-fiction book, but the Challenger Deep is actually the lowest known point on Earth. It is found in the Mariana Trench, a long gash in the floor of the Pacific Ocean. The Challenger Deep is around 10.9 km (6.77 miles) below the ocean's surface.

Mount Everest

If Mount Everest, the highest mountain on Earth, was dropped into the Challenger Deep, its top would still be around 2 km (1.2 miles) under water.

FACT 51
Only 5% of the ocean floor has been explored and mapped.

Challenger Deep

70

Unwelcoming spot

It is very challenging to explore and learn more about the deepest point on Earth because down in the Mariana Trench the pressure is over 1,000 times greater than on the surface of the water. It's difficult not to get crushed! It is also icy cold and pitch-black because it is so far away from the light and warmth of the Sun above.

FACT
52

Fewer people have been to the Mariana Trench than have been to the Moon.

Strange creatures

It seems incredible that any life could exist in the cold, dark, crushing depths of the Mariana Trench, but it does. Amphipods, pale shrimp-like animals, grow up to 30 cm (1 ft) long there—elsewhere in the ocean they are usually smaller than your finger. There are jellyfish, flatfish, worms, sea cucumbers, and all sorts of bacteria.. This gives scientists reason to believe that aliens may exist on planets where we thought the conditions made life impossible.

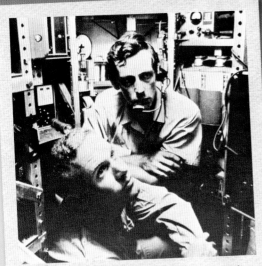

Jacques Piccard and Don Walsh inside the special craft that took them down to Challenger Deep. Cosy!

Exploring the deep

The first people to reach Challenger Deep were Jacques Piccard and Don Walsh in 1960. They spent 30 minutes there inside a special, thickly plated submarine before returning to the surface. In 2012, movie director James Cameron became the first person to go down to Challenger Deep alone, filming what he saw. Submarines without people inside have been sent down, too, to collect scientific information about its structure and the life there.

A WIND TURBINE CAN POWER YOUR HOME IN ONE SPIN

The most powerful wind turbine in the world has been built off the coast of Scotland. A single spin of its giant blades provides an average home with electricity for a whole day—without polluting the planet.

> I'm just going round in circles here!

Clean energy

We now know the planet-destroying impact of burning fuels such as coal, oil, and gas for energy. This "dirty energy" releases huge amounts of carbon dioxide into the air, adding to the greenhouse effect that traps the Sun's heat in Earth's atmosphere and warms up our planet. Clean energy such as solar power and wind power gives us electricity without making the Earth unliveable—sounds like a good idea!

FACT **54**

Wind power is not a new idea—in ancient Persia (modern Iran), windmills were used as early as 2,200 years ago!

72

Energy transfer

So how exactly do you turn wind into electricity? Well, wind is moving air and it carries "movement energy," which we call kinetic energy. When the wind passes over the turbine's blades, it pushes them and makes them spin around. Now the wind's kinetic energy has been transferred into the blades' kinetic energy, which is transferred to other moving parts inside the turbine and spins a generator that converts the kinetic energy in electrical energy.

Why so tall?

Wind turbines are getting taller, and there's a very good reason for it. Taller wind turbines are more efficient because higher up in the air the winds are stronger, so there is more potential wind energy. Higher up, there is also less turbulence—rough, disturbed movement of the air—so blades can move more smoothly, quietly and without as much wear on the machinery.

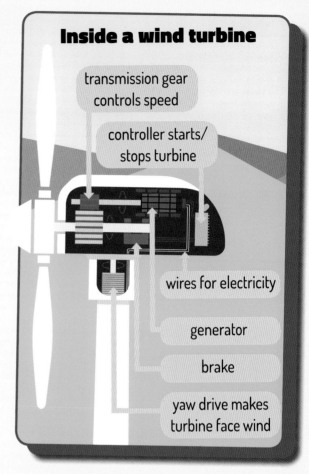

Inside a wind turbine

transmission gear controls speed

controller starts/ stops turbine

wires for electricity

generator

brake

yaw drive makes turbine face wind

Best placed

For a wind turbine to produce as much electricity as possible, it ideally needs to be somewhere with very strong winds blowing a lot of the time. Turbines are often built on the top of hills, in the middle of flat, empty plains, or out in the ocean where winds can really rage! A "wind farm" has multiple turbines built near to each other in one suitably windy spot.

This spot looks perfect! Oh wait... someone got here first!

A ROBOT HAS SET A PUZZLE-SOLVING RECORD

The Rubik's Cube, invented in 1974, is solved by moving squares around so all of the red squares are on one side, all of the blue squares are on another side, and so on. Sounds simple, but it's pretty tricky! Maybe not for robots, though ...

Rubik's records

The human record for solving a Rubik's Cube is really, really fast—just 4.22 seconds. This is even more impressive when you hear that only around 6% of the world's population is believed to be able to solve this puzzle at all! Solving a Rubik's Cube as fast as possible is called "speedcubing," a sport that has many fans and competitions all over the world.

So if this bit goes here ... then that bit must turn like that ... this is harder than it looks!

FACT 56

The fastest time someone has solved a Rubik's Cube with their feet is a mind-boggling 22 seconds.

Robot domination

However skilled some of our kind may be at "speedcubing," we puny humans can't compete with the puzzle-solving power of robots specially designed for the job. The very fastest robot can solve a Rubik's Cube—that is, work out the moves needed and then actually make the turns—in 0.38 seconds! This robot, built by students at Massachusetts Institute of Technology (MIT) in the USA, smashed the world record in 2018.

This is one of the many speedcubing robots around!

FACT
57
A twelve-year-old boy solved three Rubik's Cubes in just five minutes and six seconds—while juggling them.

Chess champions

The Rubik's Cube isn't the only game that we've lost to artificial intelligence. Back in 1997, a chess game sent shockwaves around the world when world champion Gary Kasparov lost to a computer called Deep Blue in a six-game match. Many people thought that the company which built the computer must have cheated, as it seemed too unbelievable for a computer to outsmart a super-brainy person.

Smarter and smarter

Computers and robots keep advancing all the time, getting smarter and more varied in their abilities. A security system called Captcha, which was specifically designed to be impossible for robots to solve and so was widely used, was broken in 2017 by an artificial intelligence system. Scientists are now teaching computers how to work things out for themselves and continuously evolve their thinking, by mimicking the way that human brains learn and develop.

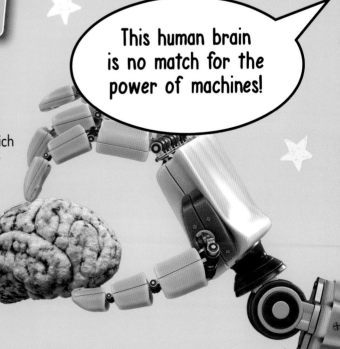

This human brain is no match for the power of machines!

75

FACT 58

SPACE DIVERS CAN FREEFALL TO EARTH

Skydiving might make a lot of people nervous, but what about space diving? Hi-tech equipment lets daredevils free-fall for miles through Earth's atmosphere before opening a parachute and landing safely on solid ground.

> Um, it's very sweet that you want to hold hands, but maybe we should open our parachutes now?

> Wheeeee!!

Daredevils

Jumping out of a plane and falling at incredible speed toward Earth, with only the few strings and fabric sheet of a parachute to keep you alive—does that sound like a nightmare or the experience of a lifetime? Either way, you're not alone. But we have the technology to get people up even higher, jumping from a point halfway to space!

FACT 59

In the USA alone, around half a million people make 3 million skydives every year.

Near-space divers

The Kármán line is an invisible marker 100 km (62 miles) above sea level, and it's where sky officially becomes space. The term "space diver" is a little misleading because no one has ever jumped from above this line, but they've gone pretty high! The very first space diver was Colonel Joseph William Kittinger II, who in 1959 went up to 23,300 m (76,400 ft) in a special balloon before falling back down to Earth.

Real dangers

High up above Earth, there is not enough oxygen to breathe in the air, so divers need to wear an oxygen supply. Two of the six people who have attempted a space dive have died as a result, both because this supply failed. Pyotr Dolgov died in 1962 after cracking his helmet, and in 1966 Nick Piantanida was left in a coma from which he never woke up after an issue with his face mask. Today's technology is stronger and safer, but space diving is still very risky.

An automatic camera captured Joseph Kittinger jumping from 31,300 m (102,800 ft) in 1960.

Record breakers

After these two tragic deaths, there was not another space dive until 2012, when expert skydiver Felix Baumgartner jumped from around 39,000 m (128,100 ft) and broke the records for highest dive and longest free fall. Baumgartner was also the first space diver to travel faster than the speed of sound on the way down. Triple threat! It was short-lived, though—just two years later, Alan Eustace jumped from a height of over 41,400 m (135,800 ft) and broke Baumgartner's records for highest dive and longest free fall.

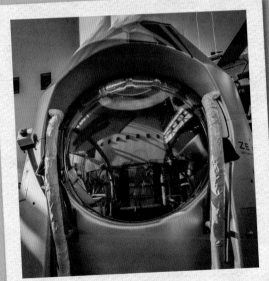

The capsule that Felix Baumgartner flew up in for his record-breaking jump.

FACT 60

For his record-breaking dive, Alan Eustace jumped from over 11 times higher than a typical skydiver today.

FACT 61

DISABILITIES CAN'T STOP ATHLETES WINNING RACES

Paralympians and Olympians are constantly breaking new records, their hard work and talent helped by advances in sport science and technology. Running blades, special artificial legs used for racing, could make humans faster than ever before.

FACT 62

Able-bodied athletes are sometimes accused of "technology doping." This term describes an athlete gaining an unfair advantage from advanced technology—anything from a swimsuit to a special bicycle design.

Parasports

Today, parasports—sports in which people with all kinds of different disabilities compete—are more popular than ever. TV audiences for major parasport events, such as the Paralympics, are growing every year as more people discover what an exciting time it is to be a parasport fan.

Wow, we're seriously hi-tech!

Look at us go!

Running blades

Athletes with one or two legs that have been amputated or missing from birth can choose to wear running blades to race. These blades don't just look cool—they are designed for serious speed, and some athletes who use them compete in races with non-disabled athletes. The blades pick up speed as they run, leading some people to question whether they give an unfair advantage over athletes who don't have artificial legs.

Hi-tech creation

Running blades are made of strips of carbon threads that are each thinner than a human hair. These strips are bound together, heated and cut to shape, to create a blade that is stronger than steel but lighter than a bag of sugar. The blade's durability is tested by a machine that quickly moves it through roughly the same number of steps that would take you from London, UK to Berlin, Germany!

Beyond blades

Many people live with one or more artificial limbs—in the USA alone, there are more than 2 million people living with limb loss. Just like non-disabled people, most people who use artificial legs are not top athletes and so probably won't ever use running blades specially designed for racing. There is a wide range of everyday artificial legs that people can use instead, and these are becoming lighter, stronger, and more comfortable as the technology keeps improving.

Walking the runway ... Or just messing about on your phone.

79

WE CAN GROW FOOD WITHOUT SOIL

Our natural world is in trouble and scientists agree we need to do all we can to fix it. But technology also offers other clever solutions to stop us going hungry in future.

Helping nature

For many years, we have been growing food in a way that really hurts the Earth, but we can still fix this damage. Some farmers have stopped using harsh chemicals that poison the soil and kill helpful animals. Some are thinking cleverly about what they plant, and how, to stop their soil blowing or washing away and their land turning into desert. Others are getting hi-tech to keep food on our tables.

FACT 64

Companies are developing robots to plant, care for, and harvest plants in indoor vertical farms without the need for humans.

A vertical farm where plants grow in trays of water rather than the ground.

We're helping!

Fishy business

There are other ways of farming that take some pressure off our damaged soil. Many vegetables, fruits, and herbs can grow with their roots in water, rather than needing to be in soil. Either the farmer puts all the nutrients that the plant needs directly into the water, or fish swim around in the water and their pee and poop gives the plants these nutrients!

Vertical farms

As the world population grows and grows, space becomes more limited. What if you could use the same amount of land and grow ten times as much food or more? In vertical farms, plants grow indoors under artificial light, in multiple levels stacked on top of each other. Farmers can control the temperature, water, and light levels in a way they can't in traditional outdoor farms, so the plants grow faster and use less water.

IF WE DIDN'T EAT MEAT OR DAIRY PRODUCTS, WE WOULD NEED ONLY A QUARTER OF THE FARMLAND TO FEED THE WORLD.

Floating farms

Most of Earth is covered in water, not land, so why not try to use some of the ocean's vast space for farming? The first ever floating farm was built in the Netherlands in 2018. It's a triple-decker building anchored to the ocean floor in the middle of the city of Rotterdam. Forty cows will live there, and the farm's top level will grow clover and grass for them to eat.

LAB-GROWN BACTERIA CAN EAT WASTE PLASTIC

There is a huge amount of plastic waste in the world, polluting our land and water. This is a huge problem because plastic doesn't really break down naturally. But what if it does, with the right bacteria on the case?

ONLY AROUND 20% OF PLASTIC IS RECYCLED, WHILE THE REST OF IT IS THROWN AWAY OR BURNED.

Plastic problem

Imagine you're walking through a supermarket, with shelves of food and drink stretching above and ahead of you. How many of the products for sale are packaged in some type of plastic? Think about how much plastic waste that adds up to, in just one supermarket! It all has to go somewhere, and although some can now be recycled there is still a lot left over ...

Mmmmm ...

Let me at it!

Yummy!

Hero bacteria

In 2016, a team of scientists in Japan found bacteria living in a waste dump that are able to "eat" PET, one of the world's most-used plastics. The bacteria break down the plastic by producing an enzyme—a natural substance that can speed up chemical reactions—known as PETase. This creates smaller plastic particles that the bacteria can absorb and use for food.

Franken-zyme

While studying these exciting Japanese bacteria, scientists in the UK accidentally created a turbo-powered version of the plastic-eating enzyme. This new "lab mutant" enzyme is able to break down PET plastic faster than the original version, and can also "eat" an alternative plastic called PEF.

This mound of PET plastic bottles would be a tasty treat for some bacteria!

FACT
66

Bakelite, invented in 1907, was the world's first synthetic plastic. That means it wasn't made from plants or animals, like earlier plastics were.

Come on, little bacteria buddies, we need your help!

Scaling up

Scientists around the world are excited about the potential of this research, although there is some way to go before the still relatively slow-eating bacteria are any match for the enormous amount of plastic waste humans produce every day. Other bacteria look like they might help us with our eco crisis, too—scientists are looking at using bacteria to generate electricity from carbon dioxide and water. Thanks, little friends!

WE CAN PUT OUT FIRES WITH SOUND

Raging wildfires kill people and animals and cause massive amounts of damage to the environment. However, fire fighters may soon have a new tool to give them some much-needed extra help.

Hotter and hotter

Wildfires are a huge problem in many areas of the world, and global warming means that they are getting worse. Around the world, the length of the wildfire season grew by almost 20% between 1978 and 2013. The hotter, drier weather linked to climate change means that it is easier for fires to start and spread quickly.

IN THE USA, UP TO 90% OF ALL WILDFIRES ARE STARTED BY PEOPLE—EITHER DELIBERATELY OR THROUGH CARELESS ACCIDENTS SUCH AS DROPPED CIGARETTE ENDS AND CAMPFIRES THAT AREN'T PUT OUT PROPERLY.

Tactical approach

It can be incredibly difficult and dangerous to put out wildfires, and spraying them with water from hoses often isn't effective. Wildfire fighters study weather patterns and track the fire's movements, acting tactically to stop it from spreading. Planes and helicopters drop water and chemicals on the flames in specially chosen areas, while people on the ground cut down trees and plants to create bare "fire lines" to contain the fire.

Sound technology

Two engineering students, Seth Robertson and Viet Tran, have built a sound-based fire extinguisher to try to take fire-fighting technology to the next level. The idea behind the invention is that because sound waves cause vibrations as they travel, they can be made to push apart burning material and the oxygen around it. Starved of oxygen, the fire dies. In tests, bassy low-frequency sounds (but not high-frequency ones) helped to put out small fires.

Earth and beyond

Robertson and Tran are developing their design for eventual use on a large scale. It is hoped that fire fighters could attach this sound extinguisher to a drone flown over a wildfire, and safely control the blaze without using vast supplies of water and chemicals. And what about beyond Earth? Putting out fires on spacecraft can be very tricky—and messy, as any material from an extinguisher flies all over the place! No clean-up with sound, though ...

Remember ... the sound extinguisher is for putting out fires, NOT for dance parties.

85

A HI-TECH SIEVE MAKES SEAWATER DRINKABLE

Have you ever found yourself thirsty at the seaside? There's water as far as you can see, but none you can drink. But scientists may have come up with a solution. They have found a way to make dirty, salty seawater safe to drink.

FACT **69**

There is evidence of people in ancient Greece and India filtering water around 4,000 years ago to make it taste better.

Deadly dehydration

Have you ever accidentally swallowed a mouthful of seawater? Yeeuuck, right?! So salty! The high levels of salt in seawater mean that it's no good for us to drink—in fact, too much of it can be deadly. Our kidneys can't make pee that is as salty as seawater, so if you keep drinking seawater you get thirstier and thirstier as you are peeing out more water than you are taking in.

Hmm, I could really do with that magic sieve right about now ...

Super sieve

Now a team of researchers based in the UK has created a sieve to take the salt out of seawater. It is made of a material called graphene oxide, with holes in it that are so small that although water particles can pass through it salt particles can't. It can also filter out other toxic particles in dirty water to make it safe for people to drink.

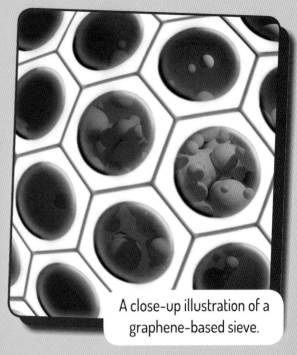

A close-up illustration of a graphene-based sieve.

Getting salty

We need lots of fresh water—water that isn't salty—to drink ourselves and to give to crops that will end up as food for people or farm animals. Around the world, but particularly in poorer countries, water salinization—fresh water becoming more salty—is becoming a big problem. One of the causes of this is climate change meaning that sea levels are rising and salty water is spreading into new areas.

Safe to drink

In parts of the world, many people still really struggle to find any water that they can safely drink. One small but mighty piece of technology to try and help solve the problem is a special straw. It filters water as you suck it up, making it safe to drink by the time it reaches your mouth! Another idea is a "drinkable book" with special tear-out pages that people use to filter dirty water.

LifeStraw is one of the water-filtering straws available that makes unappealing water safe to drink.

FACT 70
SEA ANIMALS COULD SAFELY EAT NEW PLASTICS

Levels of plastic pollution in the sea are at crisis levels, with over 100 million sea animals dying each year as a result of it. Scientists are trying to create non-toxic, biodegradable, edible plastics to help solve this.

> I mean, I'd still prefer a nice bit of squid, but thanks, I guess ...

Trashing the ocean

Every year almost 3 billion pieces of plastic pollution find their way into the ocean. There are only around 7.6 billion people alive today on Earth! This pollution gets inside sea animals and often has fatal results. In 2018, scientists found that 100% of the sea turtles they studied had plastic pollution in their bodies.

THERE IS A HUGE FLOATING ISLAND OF PLASTIC WASTE IN THE PACIFIC OCEAN THAT IS NOW AROUND TWICE THE SIZE OF FRANCE.

Mmm ... yummy?

We may know the difference between food and plastic, but for many sea animals plastic often looks, smells, and even feels like their usual food and so they eat it. And that means problems for us as well. We may not deliberately eat plastic, but if we eat fish and shellfish, there's a good chance we're swallowing at least some plastic that way.

Plant plastics

Some companies believe that we don't have to choose between plastic and the health of our planet—we just need to choose the right kind of plastic. Bioplastics are plastics made from natural materials, and they are designed to be less harmful for the environment and to break down naturally over time. However, studies have shown mixed results as to how eco-friendly they might be overall.

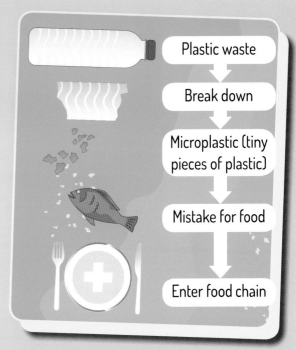

Plastic waste

↓

Break down

↓

Microplastic (tiny pieces of plastic)

↓

Mistake for food

↓

Enter food chain

Drinkable plastic?!

One company, Avani, believes it has created a plastic bag that is truly safe for animals to eat—they even claim that a person could dissolve one in hot water and safely drink it! The bag is made from a starchy root vegetable called cassava, and is designed to break down entirely within three to six months. But even this plastic bag isn't perfect. Firstly, producing any single-use item wastes a lot of energy and resources. Secondly, growing cassava for plastic takes away a food crop needed by the world's growing population. Tricky!

FACT 71

A 610 m/2,000 ft-long floating pipe, designed to trap plastic waste in the ocean, is currently in development. The idea is that these machines could become "ocean garbage trucks."

Technology can help us tackle our plastic waste issue, but we also need to cut down how much plastic we throw away.

FACT 72

SMARTER HOMES CAN HELP SAVE THE PLANET

Houses often use a lot of energy and water, which has a big impact on the environment. But what if your house could give something back? New smart technology and clever ways of building can make a huge difference.

Smartphones and homes

Smartphone apps can be a great help if we want to avoid wasting energy at home. We can turn off any forgotten lights with a swipe of a finger, or shut off the heating if it has accidentally been left on. Smart plugs can be attached to all kinds of electronic devices, so anything from a coffee maker to a laptop charger can be switched on and off through an app, too.

FACT 73

Smart home devices are part of the "Internet of Things." This is a network of objects—anything from cars to hairdryers—with computers in them, which can send and receive information.

90

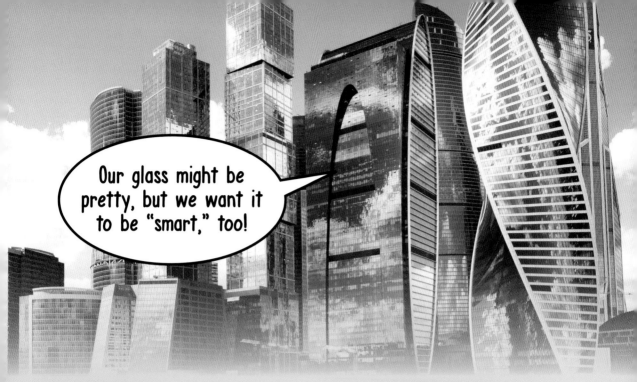

Our glass might be pretty, but we want it to be "smart," too!

Eco comforts

Many eco-friendly technologies let us enjoy our home comforts while also being kinder to our planet. For instance, some special shower heads mix jets of air with the flowing water as it comes through. You get the same lovely, high-pressure shower as always—but it is air rather than extra water that provides the pressure, so you use less water.

Hard-working walls

A lot of modern buildings have glass walls—they can look impressive and give a great view of the outside world. But what if these walls could also power your home—without you having to lift a finger? Photovoltaic glass panels capture the Sun's energy to be used for electricity and heating, as traditional black solar panels do, but you can see through them just as you would a normal pane of glass.

The Ecocapsule

Ecocapsules

A caravan or mobile home lets you travel with your home comforts at hand, but an Ecocapsule takes things one step farther ... An Ecocapsule is a small, moveable house that is designed to be totally self-sufficient. It takes energy from the sun and wind, and collects and processes rainwater. Because it doesn't need any energy or water wired or pumped in, you could live anywhere—from a beach to a mountain top!

FACT 74 — ROBOT BEES CAN HELP OUR FOOD GROW

We need bees to make our food crops grow, so you'd think we'd take better care of them. But bees are dying in huge numbers, thanks to us, so we are bringing in robots to help do the job.

FACT 75

Tiny tracker "backpacks" have been attached to bees so scientists can follow their movements and better understand why bees in certain areas are dying.

Pollinators

Around the world, three-quarters of the main food crops we grow rely on pollinators—animals that carry pollen between flowering plants so they can make seeds that grow into new plants. Although birds and mammals, such as bats, can pollinate plants, it is mostly insects that do this important work. Butterflies, moths, beetles, and others help us out a lot, but bees are the star of the pollination show.

Bees in trouble

We depend on bees' efforts for so many different fruits and vegetables, from strawberries and apples to cucumbers and potatoes, and for the cotton that our clothes are often made from—not to mention honey! But we haven't treated them very well in return.  Global warming has messed up the conditions they need to live healthily, and many farms have treated the natural world badly—including using pest-killing poisons that also destroy bees.

We give you honey and you give us poison—come on humans, that's not a fair swap!

FACT
76

People trying to keep real-life bees alive can now download and 3D-print designs for bee hives, then upload data on how their bees are doing!

Pollination

Bees carry pollen from the male part of one flower to the female part of another flower.

Robot drones

Scientists around the world have been working to create drones—remotely controlled flying robots—that they hope could step in to help if the bees continue dying out. A swarm of these robot bees could be sent out into a field or a large greenhouse, moving from flower to flower to pollinate the plants just like a bee does. Scientists have now successfully pollinated plants with a drone, without damaging the inside of the flower.

Don't give up!

It's great to know that technology may be able to help us with this sticky situation, but even the robot bee inventors have said that we need to use bees and drones together, not drones alone. Bees are part of a delicately balanced natural world, and it's not too late to work to restore it. In Europe, laws banning bee-killing chemicals and efforts to plant bee-friendly flowers have already slowed the rate at which bees are dying.

FACT 77

WE CAN GROW A HAMBURGER IN A LAB

Would you eat meat grown in a lab? It seems odd but this cultured meat, or "clean meat," might feel much more normal in future. And the environment may thank you for choosing it over traditional meat ...

The first appearance

The world's first ever lab-grown burger made its first appearance back in 2013—with a premium price tag of $330,000 (£215,000). The feedback from food critics and researchers was on the whole positive, most people agreeing that the texture was pretty good but the taste needed a bit of work. To get the burger looking right, it also had to be stained with beetroot juice, as the lab-grown meat was naturally white!

THE USA IS THE BIGGEST MEAT-EATING NATION ON EARTH, WITH EACH PERSON CONSUMING AN AVERAGE OF 100 KG (220 LB) OF MEAT IN A YEAR. THAT'S THE WEIGHT OF MORE THAN 3,300 MCDONALD'S BURGER PATTIES!

You wanted a burger? I hope you can afford me!

How do you "grow" a burger?

Well, the scientists who made the first lab-grown burger started by taking stem cells from a cow. These are special cells that have the potential to develop into different types of cell, rather than just one kind. These stem cells were given nutrients and chemicals to help them develop into muscle cells and multiply—three weeks later, there were more than a million. They formed small strips of muscle, which were processed and made into a burger!

At the moment, our big appetite for beef means huge areas of rainforest are destroyed every year to make more room for cows to graze.

OK, so ... why?!

Growing meat in a lab removes many of the concerns that can lead people to choose vegetarianism—killing animals, the conditions in which animals are kept and transported, the massive environmental impact. The few cells needed to grow the meat can be taken from a live animal, there is no need to rear animals in captivity, and scientists believe the process creates 96% less planet-warming greenhouse gas emissions than traditional meat production.

FACT 78

The first time scientists managed to take animal stem cells was from mice back in 1981.

The future of meat

One company that produces "clean meat" has said that it may be available to buy very soon. And it seems that the world is ready for it now—in the USA, where only around 3% of people are vegetarian, one in three people have said that they would be willing to eat lab-grown meat regularly or have it entirely replace traditionally farmed meat in their diet.

So, would you eat me?!

FACT 79 YOU CAN FEEL A FIRE ALARM GOING OFF

If you do not have a hearing impairment, you may never have thought about how much we are alerted to danger by sounds alone. Alarms, sirens, and horns all rely on hearing—but electronic devices and smart technology can change that.

FACT 80

The first electric hearing aid was created in 1898, but as long as 800 years ago people used hollow animal horns to funnel sound into their ears and hear more clearly.

Sounding the alarm

Have you ever been woken up by a fire alarm and had to get dressed and move outside to a safe place? It can be annoying or scary, but what if you hadn't been able to hear the alarm at all? If fire alarm systems do not include a way for people with hearing impairments to be alerted to the danger, it could be deadly.

Waking up

An adapted fire alarm system alerts people with hearing impairments to danger with bright flashing lights, and a vibrating pad that is placed under the pillow for when they are asleep. This same technology is used to wake people up in less extreme circumstances, too—adapted alarm clocks use a strong vibration rather than a loud noise.

Disability and technology

One way of thinking about disability is that additional difficulty in a person's life is not caused by this difference but by our society's refusal to respond to their different needs. Technology can make a huge difference in the lives of people with disabilities. For example, for people with a hearing impairment, the standard vibration settings on smartphones and smartwatches can be really helpful—and don't require fiddly or expensive adaptation.

Video call technology means people can now use sign language to communicate with others across the world.

Smartphones and smartwatches

There are apps for smartphones and smartwatches specially designed for hearing-impaired users. For example, there is an app in which you program in sounds from around the home such as a doorbell, so that when it goes off a picture pops up on your phone or watch, with a vibration alert, to let you know.

BUMPY LIDS HELP STOP FOOD WASTE

Food waste is a huge problem in many countries and "Use By" labels often encourage people to throw away food that is still perfectly good and safe to eat. But your food packaging might be about to get smarter ...

Expiry dates

We have only really had Best Before, Use By, Sell By, and other similar labels on our food since the 1970s, and the system isn't as exact a science as many people assume it is. In fact, in many cases these kinds of labels describe when the food is best to eat rather than anything to do with safety.

Hmm, I don't know if I can trust you any more ...

Safe or sorry?

Obviously we all want to make sure that the food we're eating is safe and hasn't gone bad, but how long something stays fresh depends on many different things—including the temperature of your fridge. The printed "Use By" and similar dates are printed on every item coming through at the same time, and therefore can't take this difference into account, so they may tell you not to eat foods that are still totally fine.

Mimica Touch

A new technology, the Mimica Touch, doesn't go by the date that something is produced but rather by its current state. It is "bio-active," which means that it tells us whether an item of food is safe to eat by mimicking the natural changes that happen when that particular food starts to go bad. Because it is based on reality rather than guessing, it means that you don't waste food unnecessarily.

Bumpy or smooth?

Containers with Mimica Touch technology have a layer of gelatine in the lid, which goes bumpy when the food inside the container is spoiled. So if you run your finger over the Mimica Touch and it feels smooth, go ahead and eat up! If it feels bumpy, it's time to throw away the food inside.

Mimica Touch label

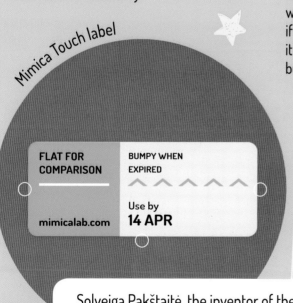

FLAT FOR COMPARISON	BUMPY WHEN EXPIRED
mimicalab.com	∧ ∧ ∧ ∧ ∧ Use by 14 APR

Solveiga Pakštaitė, the inventor of the Mimica Touch label, won the important UK James Dyson design award for her invention at the age of just 22!

AIR POLLUTION CAN BE MADE INTO JEWELS

Air pollution is a huge problem in cities all over the world, causing health issues and early deaths for many. Could we really turn something as ugly as that into a beautiful ring or pendant?

Smog Tower

The Smog Tower, developed by the design lab Studio Roosegaarde in the Netherlands, sucks in pollution from the surrounding area and pushes out clean air for people to breathe. These pollution-guzzling towers are already installed in the Netherlands, Poland, and four cities in China. Their creators have said that each tower can clean around 3.5 million cubic m (124 million cubic ft) of air every day—that's 1,400 Olympic-sized swimming pools of fresh air!

> Who wants a diamond ring when they could have a stone made from pollution?

FACT 83

Indoor air pollution, mostly in places where people use very old-fashioned cooking technology, causes around 4 million people to die too early each year.

100

Stylish smog

Once the pollution particles from the air have been safely captured in the Smog Towers, they are squeezed tightly together into a sort of gemstone! This can be set in rings, pendants—whatever you want, really! The rings have proved popular with couples getting married—mining diamonds for the traditional glittering engagement ring can cause terrible harm to the environment, so some prefer to try to help the environment instead by choosing a "smog ring!"

Deadly air

In cities, traffic is a big part of our air pollution problems. Many cars and other vehicles pump out toxic fumes that hurt the environment and—more immediately—our health. Studio Roosegaarde has developed an air-cleaning bicycle to try to help with this issue. The bicycle takes in polluted air, cleans it, and gives the cyclist this clean air. The bicycles have been tested in Shanghai, a city in China with very high air pollution levels.

ACROSS THE WORLD, AROUND 93% OF CHILDREN UNDER THE AGE OF 15 BREATHE AIR SO POLLUTED THAT IT PUTS THEIR HEALTH AND DEVELOPMENT AT SERIOUS RISK.

Pollution particles captured by the Smog Tower.

Clean break

It is a shocking reality that over 95% of the world's population breathes dangerously polluted air. Airlabs, a Danish company, has used air-filtering technology to create "clean air hotspots" in London, UK, a city with very high levels of air pollution. Their special bench and bus stops are designed to give a taster of the better-quality air we should all be breathing.

FACT 84 WE CAN USE DNA TO STORE DATA

The massive rise of computers and the internet over the last few decades has changed the world. But it has also created a LOT of data. Where are we going to put it all? DNA might be the answer.

FACT 85

If all the world's data was stored as DNA, it would weigh less than two elephants, and could be moved around on the back of a truck.

Small and stable

DNA is incredibly good at storing a lot of complex information in a very small space and it remains stable for thousands of years. At the moment, most digital data in archives is stored on magnetic tape, which is the cheapest current option but takes up quite a lot of space and it doesn't last that long—the data will disappear after ten years, so the tape has to be renewed regularly.

One code to another

Digital data files are written in binary code, a series of 0s and 1s, and DNA has its own sort of code made of "bases" represented by the letters A, G, C, and T. In a DNA strand, these bases are arranged in pairs, and digital data can be mapped onto these base pairs. By building a DNA strand with a particular sequence of base pairs, you can store the data in the strand in the right order.

When you want to retrieve the data, you read the DNA with a special machine and translate it back into binary code.

We're all full up, no more!

Data overload

By 2025, experts think that every year we will produce 36 times the amount of data that was created from the beginning of human existence up until 2013! If we carry on with the same storage methods that we use today, there won't be anywhere near enough space for all this data. We need to find a solution fast, and DNA seems like one of the best options.

IN 2017, SCIENTISTS STORED TWO MUSIC RECORDINGS IN DNA, THEN DECODED THEM AGAIN AND PLAYED THEM BACK WITHOUT ANY LOSS OF QUALITY.

Cloud storage

What about "the cloud?" That magical internet space where you can back up or store your files so you don't have to worry about keeping them on your devices? Well, the cloud still relies on real-world computers to store all this data! Cloud storage companies need huge buildings to store all their equipment. At the moment they just keep expanding into new buildings, but there will come a point quite soon where it gets really tricky to find the space!

FACT 86

OUR FOOTSTEPS COULD KEEP CITIES LIT UP

Walking and cycling are healthy, eco-friendly ways to get around. Much better than petrol and diesel cars that pollute everyone's air. And better still if we can use technology to generate clean energy at the same time ...

Power walking

Major cities around the world use a lot of energy staying lit up day and night, and have a lot of people walking through their streets. Las Vegas, a city known for its dazzling lights and glitzy sparkle, has found a way to make the two work together. Special paving tiles have been laid in some of the busiest parts of Las Vegas, and every time someone steps on them the energy from this pushing-down movement is captured and transferred to surrounding street lights to power them.

We've got real people power!

Green lighting

The company that makes this footstep-powered lighting system says that more than 300 million street lights around the world are producing a total of more than 100 million tons of carbon dioxide. If these lights could become carbon-neutral by being powered by clean, renewable energy, it would have the same effect as taking more than 19 million cars off the road.

Only when needed

As well as working out how to generate power cleanly, we are also looking at how to waste less of it. Smart streetlight systems have sensors so they can tell when people are approaching, and if there is no one around they turn off or dim their light. This can save a huge amount of energy, and it has other benefits—bright lights at night can confuse and harm animals, and this minimizes the disruption.

Solar cycle paths

In the Netherlands, the SolaRoad bicycle path is made of solar panels covered with layers of toughened glass and other materials to make the surface suitable for cycling. A solar path such as this one captures energy from the Sun to generate clean, sustainable power while also providing a safe route for cyclists to get around—hopefully persuading more people to leave their polluting cars at home. That's a double win!

Don't forget about pedal power!

SPORTSWEAR CAN WARN ATHLETES OF DANGER

Athletes can push their bodies to do incredible things, but sometimes this can put them in serious danger. Technology can help keep them safe by picking up on warning signs that are invisible to us.

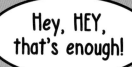

Hey, HEY, that's enough!

Smart fabrics

One important area of "safety sportswear" is smart fabrics that can measure changes in an athlete's body as they train or perform. There are all sorts of designs available to monitor the wearer's heart rate and breathing patterns, and this data can be read on a smartphone or special device. It can tell athletes, and their coaches, when they might be training dangerously hard.

Yeah, listen to us, we're really smart.

FACT 88

Smart sportswear isn't just about saving lives, it can also improve athletes' performance. Smart shorts can give runners all kinds of information about their pace and technique, which can prevent injury and improve skill level.

Concussion sensors

For athletes who take part in high-contact sports such as football, rugby, and boxing, concussion is a very real danger. Concussion is a temporary brain injury caused by a blow to the head, and over time multiple concussions could result in serious, permanent brain damage. Concussion sensors—built into helmets, headbands, mouthguards, and wearable patches—detect when a player has been hit hard enough to be at risk.

Helping us help ourselves

Many athletes don't realize they have a concussion at first, or don't seek treatment when they have symptoms because they don't want to be seen as "weak." The concussion sensor gives an objective measurement, sent directly to a person responsible for athletes' wellbeing, so it can help with this issue. If a player suffers a lot of concussions, they can be trained to change their technique to keep themselves safer from injury.

Personalized solutions

In 2018, living legend Serena Williams wore a fitted black bodysuit while playing in the French Open tennis tournament. The organizers, unimpressed by her non-traditional outfit, announced that they would be changing the dress code to ban bodysuits in future. But this suit wasn't just a fashion choice—it was designed to protect Williams from serious health issues. The suit helped stop dangerous blood clots from forming, a problem that had threatened Williams's life during her pregnancy the year before.

Serena Williams in her potentially life-saving bodysuit.

FACT 89

YOU CAN PRINT YOUR DINNER

Many people today want to eat healthily but find it hard to make time in their busy lives to prepare and cook meals from scratch. What if a 3D printer could do the hard work for you?

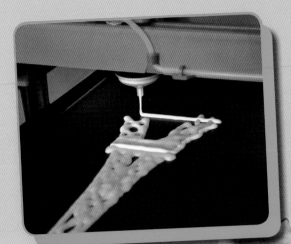

Helping hand

A 3D food printer can perfectly pipe out different foods, from veggie burgers and fresh pasta to pizzas and fun, shaped cookies. The ingredients need to be soft enough to be printed through the nozzles, so you sometimes need to mix foods into a smooth texture before adding them to the machine. Some 3D printers in development cook the food as well, so it's a one-stop meal machine!

Yes indeed! I am a castle made of hummus!

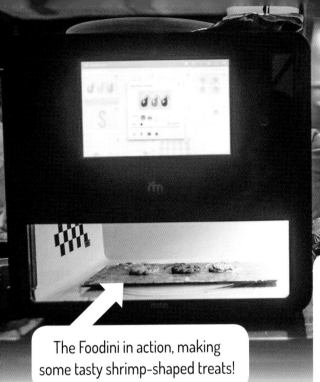

The Foodini in action, making some tasty shrimp-shaped treats!

Foodini

The Foodini is a 3D food printer designed for restaurants and home kitchens. You load fresh ingredients into stainless steel capsules, and they are squeezed through a nozzle and printed in your chosen design below. Imagine an icing bag, like you'd use to decorate a cake, but instead of drawing patterns by hand you program a machine to put the icing in exactly the right place—and build up layers to create 3D shapes.

Top chefs

Restaurants and catering companies have shown a lot of interest in 3D food printing, as it can create complicated and technically difficult designs quickly and precisely. Chefs may be incredibly skillful but they are not machines, and so it is impossible for them to recreate intricate patterns perfectly every single time—not so for a 3D food printer! Paco Pérez, one of the world's top chefs and a Foodini fan, has said, "Creativity is shaped by what technology can do."

Printing in space

NASA is looking at how to use 3D food printing to provide better meals for astronauts while they are in space. Rather than the freeze-dried, pre-packaged "space food" that they currently eat day after day, 3D-printed food could offer some tasty variety—without the risk of half-cooked food floating around inside the spacecraft!

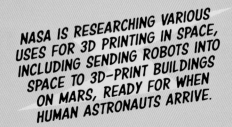

NASA IS RESEARCHING VARIOUS USES FOR 3D PRINTING IN SPACE, INCLUDING SENDING ROBOTS INTO SPACE TO 3D-PRINT BUILDINGS ON MARS, READY FOR WHEN HUMAN ASTRONAUTS ARRIVE.

FACT 90 PEOPLE HAVE TAKEN VACATIONS IN SPACE

Space tourism is a dream for many, but for a very few people it has already become a reality. Between 2001 and 2009, seven people paid around $20-40 million to travel into space.

Dream destination

If you could travel anywhere on Earth, where would you go? What about if you didn't have to limit yourself to Earth? There are different kinds of space tourism to choose from—would you rather travel up to the edge of space, circle all the way around the Earth, or take a longer trip all the way to the Moon? Several companies hope to offer this opportunity of a lifetime within just a few years.

FACT 91

Dennis Tito, a multi-millionaire engineer from the USA, became the world's first-ever space tourist in 2001 when he funded his own eight-day vacation visiting the International Space Station.

> I tell you what's really out of this world—how relaxed I feel right now. Aaaahhh.

Working vacation

So far, the only company to take paying customers into space is Space Adventures, based in Virginia, USA. It worked with Roscosmos, the Russian space agency, to get these space tourists a place aboard spacecraft heading up to the International Space Station with working astronauts. The term "space tourism" is resented by those who went into space this way, as they insist that they were asked to carry out useful research.

I know we're supposed to be helping the scientists, but come on— we're on vacation!

Space setbacks

In 2009, space tourism took a blow when Roscosmos stopped offering up places in their spacecraft. The number of astronauts living aboard the International Space Station had doubled, from three to six, and they needed more space to take up these extra crew members. Other planned tourist trips by different companies since 2009 have been cancelled or postponed for all sorts of reasons, from safety concerns to money problems.

Super-luxe space

There are still several well-funded commercial projects hoping to revive space tourism, and take it further than ever before, within the next few years. Whereas space tourists have so far hitched a ride on existing missions, companies are trying to create a purpose-built, far more comfortable experience for their future customers. The super-rich people they hope to have on board are used to luxury, daaarling! Why should space be any different?

Oh no, are we all out of the space smoked salmon?

I can't hear you, I'm in the space jacuzzi!

YOU COULD TAKE A FLYING CAR TO SCHOOL

Is it a bird? Is it a plane? No, it's you in the passenger seat of your family's flying car, on the way to school! It sounds too cool to be true, but flying cars actually already exist ...

Door to door

Apart from the obvious "wow" value, what is the point of a flying car? Well, for one thing, you can travel door to door over long distances without having to worry about catching your plane or parking your car. Flying cars are designed not to have to use a runway to take off and land, so if you aren't close to an airport it's not a problem. Plus, you fly right over the traffic jams!

LEGENDARY CAR MANUFACTURER HENRY FORD IS REPORTED TO HAVE SAID, BACK IN 1940, "MARK MY WORDS: A COMBINATION AIRPLANE AND MOTORCAR IS COMING. YOU MAY SMILE, BUT IT WILL COME."

Am I still dreaming? No, this really is our morning journey now!

Different companies are now developing flying cars, in a range of futuristic designs

Making it official

A flying car has now been developed that is officially recognized as a light aircraft and is also legal to drive on the road. This is very important, because a flying car isn't much good if you can't legally drive or fly it anywhere! The Transition is a two-seater car with wings that fold out when you're ready to take to the skies, and it takes less than a minute to switch between its driving and flying modes.

Driver, pilot, or passenger?

At the moment, anyone wanting to get behind the wheel of a flying car must be both a licensed driver and a licensed pilot. However, there are plans for cars to be self-flying and self-driving in the future, so the entire journey—whether by road or sky—would be entirely controlled by computers. Until then? If you can't drive a flying car yourself, you could hop in a "sky taxi"—another idea currently in development.

Safety first

It is statistically very safe to travel by plane, but will it stay that way with thousands—or some day maybe millions—of flying cars all zipping through the air at once?! Hi-tech safety features are planned to help with this—for example, the car's computer system automatically avoiding other vehicles in the air. But as the number of active flying cars grows, there will need to be clear systems in place to keep the skies safe.

Imagine this many cars flying through the sky!

No, thanks!

YOU COULD PRINT A NEW HOUSE

For most people, a house is the most expensive thing they'll ever buy. It takes months to build a new house, involving a lot of skilled work and preparation. But what if you could just print one instead?

From screen to home

So how exactly do you print a house? Well, first you have to design it on a computer. Then you give digital instructions to a 3D printer to bring it to life by printing it in layers of material—often plastics, or cement mixed with other materials. As the layers build up from the floor, the walls are built—and the program leaves spaces for doors and windows. Ta da!

CHARLES HULL WAS THE FIRST PERSON TO CREATE A WORKING 3D PRINTER, BACK IN 1983.

Yes, that's the idea, but we will need it quite a lot bigger ...

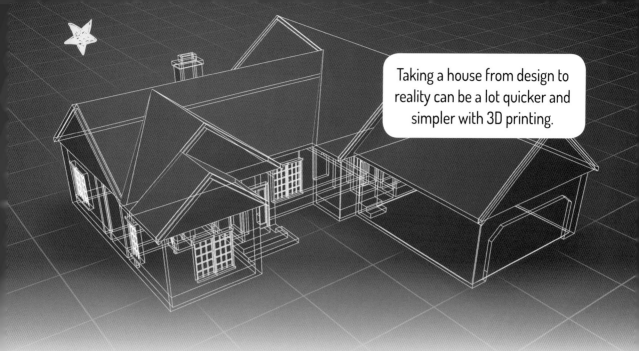

Taking a house from design to reality can be a lot quicker and simpler with 3D printing.

Better building?

Many believe that 3D printing could be the realistic future of house-building. It can be quicker, cheaper, and more eco-friendly than current building methods, which often create large amounts of waste and pollution. Companies all around the world are racing to get ahead of each other, and the technology is improving and becoming more affordable all the time.

Moving in

In 2018, the Ramdanis of Nantes, France, became the first family in the world to move into a 3D-printed house. It took only 54 hours to print, although it was then another four months before workers finished the house by adding the roof and all the windows and doors. At a total cost of around $221,000 (£176,000), it cost 20% less than if it was built through traditional means.

Emergency shelter

In 2018, a company in the USA printed a single-level house in under 24 hours for only $4,000 (£3,180). Some people might think only of the profits to be made with housing this cheap to produce, but others see the good this technology could do in the world. 3D printers could quickly create safe, low-cost housing for refugees and migrants fleeing home, survivors of natural disasters, and other homeless people.

3D-printed house

115

FACT 94
COMPUTERS CAN THINK FOR THEMSELVES

A common fear about technology is that super-advanced computers will start thinking for themselves, without needing humans ... Well, not to worry anyone, but they already can!

FACT 95

The Turing test is designed to measure how intelligent a computer seems. To pass this test, a computer must convince a human that they are talking to another human.

Flatworm puzzle

In 2018, artificial intelligence (AI) had a big win—in just three days, a computer managed to solve a mystery that had defeated scientists for around 100 years! The problem in question was working out how a flatworm can regenerate into new living creatures when it is sliced into pieces. Scientists couldn't understand the genetic reason for this ability—until AI came along ...

Hey, stop stealing my ideas!

Human help

Although it took the computer only a short time to solve the flatworm problem, scientists spent years developing the program that gave it the information and processes to be able to do so. This enabled the AI to run independently through all the possible models for a flatworm's genetic network which might make regeneration possible, eventually finding one that fitted with the results of scientists' studies so far.

Helping humans

Flatworms are just the beginning, though ... AI can help us with all sorts of things, from medicine to the environment, and self-teaching systems can keep learning and improving over time. One AI system can already predict more accurately than the best existing model where aftershocks (mini-earthquakes) will take place after a main earthquake. Humans give it the data, but it finds patterns and relationships that humans can't manage to spot.

AI brainpower

At the heart of these advanced, self-evolving AI systems are artificial neural networks, computer systems whose design is inspired by the human brain and nervous system. Our brain contains many billions of neurons—tiny parts that are connected to each other in lots of complicated ways at once. An artificial neural network aims to mimic this inter-connectedness so that a computer can learn for itself as humans do, by making new links and developing new ideas.

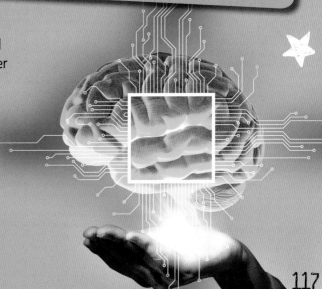

ROBOT CUBES HAVE SELF-TRANSFORMING POWERS

In the *Transformers* series, alien robots can turn themselves into vehicles and wild animals and then back into their stand-up fighting forms at a moment's notice. But Earth might now have its own army of self-assembling robots ...

We can do anything!

No need to rub it in ...

Modular robots

Most robots have a fixed shape—they might be tall and human-like, small and round, or take the form of one giant arm. This is because they are usually designed for a particular purpose, and their form is perfectly suited to carrying that out. However, modular robots are made up of parts that can be arranged in different ways to change their shape. This means they can adapt to perform all sorts of tasks in a range of different situations.

M-Blocks can form all sorts of shapes and structures. In future, advanced versions might be used for building furniture, scaffolding, and heavy equipment.

M-Blocks

At Massachusetts Institute of Technology (MIT) in the USA, a team is developing a modular robotic system based on cubes called M-Blocks. Each robotic cube can move itself around—zipping along the ground, climbing over other M-Blocks, and even jumping into the air. The mechanism ,that creates this movement is inside the cube, so M-Blocks can easily stack and create all sorts of shapes without extra arms, wheels, or other parts getting in the way.

Sticking together

The M-Blocks have magnets on all six faces, and magnets along the edges of each face too. These edge magnets can roll back and forth, and their special design enables the cubes to latch on to—and rotate around—each other. The cubes can join their faces or edges together in any way, rather than certain parts needing to line up exactly, which makes things much simpler when they form into different shapes.

Magnet power!

Thinking for themselves

At the moment, the M-Blocks are individually controlled by a person's instructions, sent wirelessly to each cube. John Romanishin, who created the M-Blocks with Daniela Rus and Kyle Gilpin, hopes that in future the cubes will be able to work out for themselves how to fit together to make a certain shape: "We want hundreds of cubes, scattered randomly across the floor, to be able to identify each other [and] transform into a chair, or a ladder, or a desk, on demand." Pretty cool!

FACT 97 INVISIBILITY CLOAKS ARE REAL

It sounds like something from a fantasy book or a comic, but scientists have actually found a way to hide 3D objects by draping them with a super-thin invisibility cloak.

I mean, I don't want to complain, but it would be a lot more useful if it was just a little longer ...

Real-life magic

If you're a fan of a certain young wizard with a lightning-shaped scar on his forehead, you should be familiar with the idea of an invisibility cloak. It's pretty simple—you throw it over yourself and all of a sudden you vanish from sight. But the real-life technology that can make invisibility cloaks a reality is pretty cutting-edge, and at the moment the cloaks are far too small for anyone to wear.

Trick of the light

Most of the time, we see things because light has reflected off them and into our eyes. In order to make an object invisible, scientists are trying to disrupt this process and divert the light waves away so that the object cannot be seen—not with our human eyes, at least. The invisibility cloak makes light reflect off an object as it would off a flat mirror, no matter what shape it is. So just as you could not see an object behind a mirror, so you cannot see what is behind the invisibilty cloak.

> Just because I'm invisible doesn't mean I can't still look fabulous!

Scaling up

At the moment, an invisibility cloak works on only a teeny-tiny scale—the cloak itself is around 1,000 times thinner than a human hair. It's got a big-time sense of glamour, though—it's made of tiny blocks of gold! It can also be switched "on" and "off"—from invisible to visible—by changing the way the particles in the cloak vibrate. Scientists are confident that they can scale up the technology for bigger objects—exciting!

Rochester Cloak

In fact, scientists have come up with more than one way to make objects appear invisible. In 2014, at the University of Rochester, John Howell and Joseph Choi built the "Rochester Cloak." This device, which can be made with cheap, everyday materials, uses four lenses in a special arrangement to hide an object from view while showing the image behind it. In tests, the Rochester Cloak successfully made a hand, a face, and a ruler appear invisible.

> Haha, I can park my invisible car wherever I want!

YOUR PHONE COULD HEAL ITS CRACKED SCREEN

It's annoying when something gets broken and needs to be fixed, but it can also sometimes be really dangerous and difficult to do. Scientists are making life easier for all of us by creating materials that don't need our help at all!

Self-healing glass

If you've ever cracked a phone screen and had to peer through an annoying spider's web of broken glass, you'll probably have wished for a self-healing screen. Well, in 2017, a team of scientists announced that they'd found the solution—they'd created glass that could fix any cracks in its surface with the help of just a little pressure from your fingertips. Nice!

> Hey, don't panic, I'll fix myself! Yikes, at least one of us is good in a crisis ...

Polymers

Most self-healing materials include polymers, which are large molecules made up of lots of repeating smaller parts. Polymers aren't anything new in science—man-made polymers include common, well-known materials such as PVC, polystyrene, Teflon™, and nylon. They even exist in nature—DNA is a polymer! A polymer is great for self-healing technology because when its bonds are broken it can easily make new, different ones to regain its strength.

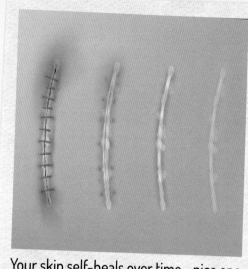

Your skin self-heals over time—nice one, hi-tech body!

Natural healing

If you cut yourself, your skin will heal itself by knitting together a layer of skin over the top of the wound. Self-healing is very important for living things, and scientists have actually used living bacteria to make self-healing concrete. When this special concrete cracks, the bacteria inside are exposed to air and water. They create a hard substance called calcite, which fills in the cracks.

FACT
99

The bacteria in self-healing concrete can stay alive but inactive for up to 200 years, ready to jump to attention when needed.

Safety first

Self-healing materials are really useful because they can fix damage that is really hard for humans to spot but that could potentially be very dangerous. An almost invisibly tiny break in the side of a plane could tear wide open if not noticed soon enough, and the thinnest of cracks in walls under pressure could eventually lead to a building's collapse. With the power of self-healing materials, tiny problems are fixed before they ever become big ones.

MIND-CONTROLLED ROBOT ARMS ALREADY EXIST

In 2017 Johnny Matheny, who lost his arm to cancer twelve years earlier, became the first person to live with a mind-controlled robotic arm. He thinks of what he wants his arm to do and, amazingly, the arm just does it.

FACT 101

The Ancient Egyptians were the first people known to use prosthetic technology. We have found artificial toes from over 2,500 years ago, made from a kind of papier maché, which scientists think helped the wearer to walk.

Better and better

For a long time, the focus of prosthetic technology—that is, artificial body parts—seems to have been on making someone look as much like everyone else as possible rather than on comfort and usability. But over time ideas about disabilities have evolved alongside the available technology, and the most advanced prosthetics are designed to feel—rather than look—as natural as possible.

Moving parts

The human hand is incredibly complex and its movement is very difficult to replicate. Simpler moving prosthetics often have a "pincer" gripping movement to pick up and hold objects. More advanced "myoelectric" prosthetics are controlled by the electrical signals sent naturally by muscles in the remainder of a limb. These signals are picked up by sensors in the prosthetic, which instruct electrical motors to move the joints—curling a fingertip, turning a wrist, bending an elbow, and more.

Next step

The robotic arm that Johnny Matheny uses is called a Modular Prosthetic Limb (MPL), and he is living independently with it as part of its ongoing development phase. He can't get the arm wet or drive while wearing it, but otherwise it can function much like his original arm. The MPL is also capable of connecting directly to the brain, so the aim is for its wearer to be able to actually feel with it—to have a sense of touch. Wow!

SCIENTISTS IN JAPAN HAVE SUCCESSFULLY TESTED A ROBOTIC THIRD ARM THAT YOU CAN USE IN ADDITION TO TWO ARMS. IMAGINE THE JUGGLING POSSIBILITIES!

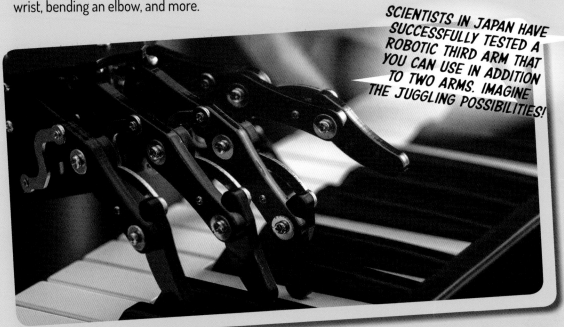

Revolution and evolution

Many people now have parts of their body that they weren't born with, artificial bits that help their bodies work better. Tooth implants are fixed into the jawbone to replace damaged and missing teeth; worn-out hip and knee joints are replaced with metal, ceramic, or plastic implants; electrical devices called pacemakers are fitted inside your chest to help your heart beat steadily. All this medical technology was once revolutionary, but now it's commonplace—the robotic arm may also be some day.

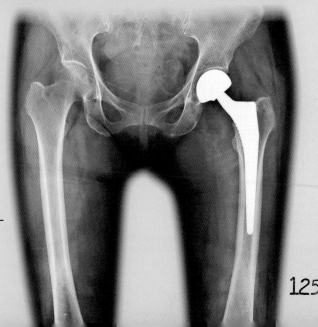

Glossary

3D printer A machine that creates three-dimensional objects, usually by stacking layers of material on top of each other.

accessibility Designing places, objects, and systems in a way that means everyone can use them, whether they have a disability or not.

antenna A rod, dish, or other structure by which radio signals are sent out or received.

artificial intelligence The ability of computer systems to seem to think for themselves, using reason and making decisions, in a way that we normally associate with human intelligence.

bacteria Tiny single-cell life forms that can cause disease and which are too small to see with your eyes alone, .

binary code A coding system in which binary numbers (zeroes and ones) are used to program a digital computer.

biodegradable Describes a material that breaks down naturally and without harming the environment.

biometric Data about people's bodies that can be usefully measured and analyzed, and used to identify people uniquely.

bionic Describes an artificial body part, usually one that uses electronics.

bioplastic A type of plastic that is made from natural materials and breaks down over time.

carbon-neutral When making or doing something doesn't release any extra carbon dioxide into Earth's atmosphere.

CCTV Closed-circuit television, in which video from cameras is sent to a limited number of screens. It is used by the police and for security systems.

concussion A temporary brain injury that is caused by a knock to the head, and which can make you sleepy and confused.

defibrillator A machine that gives an electric shock to help bring your heartbeat back to a normal rhythm.

diabetes A serious health condition related to the amount of sugar in someone's blood.

DNA Deoxyribonucleic acid (DNA) is a substance found in the cells of nearly all living things. It carries information about how a living thing looks, behaves, and so on.

drone A flying robot that can be remote-controlled rather than needing a pilot on board.

greenhouse effect The process that is warming up the Earth, in which gases trap the Sun's heat so not enough of it escapes back out into space.

hearing impairment Describes when someone cannot hear sound, or can only partly hear it.

hyperloop An ultra-high-speed overground form of transport, in which floating pods shoot through high-pressure tubes.

infrared Invisible waves that are longer than visible red light waves but shorter than microwaves.

infrastructure The basic systems needed for a society to work well, such as roads and water supply.

insecticide A poisonous substance used to kill insects.

International Space Station An artificial satellite that circles around Earth. Astronauts from all over the world live on board and carry out scientific experiments.

Internet of Things A network of objects (for example, refrigerators or microwaves) that each contain a computer which can send and receive information.

laboratory A place where scientists carry out experiments.

laser A device that gives out an intense beam of light.

LED A light-emitting diode, an electric device that gives off a bright light.

migrant Someone who moves to another country, especially for work and better living conditions.

nanotechnology Technology that deals with extremely small things.

paralyzed Describes when someone can't move a certain part, or multiple parts, of their body.

photovoltaic glass Glass that includes solar cells, which capture energy from the Sun to be used for electricity.

pollution A substance that is released into the environment and is harmful to living things and our planet.

prosthetic Describing an artificial body part.

quadstick A mouth-operated game controller.

radar Using radio waves to find out where faraway objects are and how they are moving. The waves are sent out and bounce off objects, then are picked up again.

refugee A person forced to leave their country to escape serious danger.

renewable energy Energy from a source that doesn't run out, such as wind or solar power.

satellite Any object orbiting, or moving around, a planet. Artificial (man-made) satellites are machines that orbit around Earth, and are often used for phone and TV technology.

scalpel A knife with a small, sharp blade, often used by doctors performing surgery.

sensor A device that detects, measures, or records an external activity or event.

skyscraper A very tall building.

smartphone A phone that can be used for many functions, like a handheld computer.

software The programs and operating systems used by a computer.

solar power Energy that has been captured from the Sun and which can be used for heat and electricity.

stealth plane A plane designed not to be spotted as it flies or picked up by detection systems such as radar.

stem cell A type of cell that can develop into many different cell types.

supersonic Faster than the speed of sound.

telescope A device that collects light or other radiations from space and uses them to create a bright, clear image.

transfusion The process of transferring donated blood, or other fluid, from one person or animal to another.

turbine A machine for producing power, which has a rotating part that is turned by flowing wind, water, or another gas or liquid.

virtual reality An interactive experience that resembles a version of our world but which is created by a computer.

wildfire A large fire that spreads quickly and uncontrollably through natural areas.

Index

3D printing 42–43, 48–49, 57, 93, 108–9, 114–15

age process 54–55
air pollution 25, 100–1
AlterEgo 33
apps 90, 97
artificial intelligence 5, 75, 116–17
astronauts 11, 42, 109, 111

bacteria 47, 71, 82–83, 123
Baumgartner, Felix 77
bees 92–93
bicycles 17, 101, 105
Bloodhound SSC 63
brain 14, 24, 33, 56–57, 75 107, 117, 125
Browning, Richard 8–9
buildings 10, 17, 64–65, 81, 90–91, 103, 109, 114–15, 119, 123
Burj Khalifa 64, 65
businesses 37, 59

cameras 4, 10, 11, 13, 25, 28, 29, 37, 38, 77
Cameron, James 71
cars 62–63, 90, 101, 104, 105, 112–13
Challenger Deep 70–71
chemicals 40, 41, 47, 59, 80, 83, 85, 93, 95
children 23, 31, 41, 51, 55, 57, 101
Choi, Joseph 121
cities 17, 28–29, 64, 81, 100, 101, 104–5
climate change 25, 84, 87
clothing 14, 93, 106–7
computers 24, 25, 26, 32–33, 37, 49, 56, 57, 75,90, 102, 103, 113, 114, 116–17
Concorde 67
criminals 13, 15, 28, 29

data 26, 27, 29, 93, 102–3, 106, 117
disabilities 16–17, 78–79, 96–97, 124
DNA 54, 60–61, 102–3, 123
Dolgov, Pyotr 77
drones 4–5, 10–11, 85, 93

eco-friendly 89, 91, 104, 115
Ecocapsule 91
education 23, 31
electricity 5, 17, 33, 46, 72, 73, 83, 91, 96, 125
electronics 12, 26, 29, 51, 90, 96
energy 68, 72–73, 89, 90, 91, 104–5
environment 24, 38, 84, 89, 90, 94, 95, 101, 117
Eustace, Alan 77
EyeMine 38

facial recognition 5, 13, 15, 23, 29
farming 80–81, 87, 93, 95
Feynman, Richard 58

fire 11, 84–85, 96–97
fish 81, 89
flying 6, 8–9, 10, 11, 66–67, 93, 112–13
food 11, 33, 80–81, 82, 83, 87, 89, 92–93, 94–95, 98–99, 108–9
Foodini 109

hamburger 94–95
health 11, 23, 31, 39, 40–41, 44–45, 46–47, 48–49, 50–51, 52–53, 57, 58–59, 60–61, 100, 101, 106–7
houses 72, 90–91, 114–15
Howell, John 121
Hubble Telescope 68
Hull, Charles 114
Human Genome Project 61
hyperloop 20–21

iKnife 46–47
International Space Station 42, 110, 111
internet 24, 26–27, 30, 31, 34–35, 45, 90, 102, 103
invisibility 6–7, 15, 40–41, 120–21

Jeddah Tower 65

Kasparov, Gary 75
Kindleysides, Simon 19
Kittinger II, Colonel Joseph William 77

Li-Fi 26–27
LifeStraw 87
light 26, 27, 51, 56, 68, 69, 71, 81, 90, 97, 104–5, 121
Lomas, Claire 18

machines 55, 79, 89, 103, 108, 109
Mariana Trench 70–71
Matheny, Johnny 124–25
meat 81, 94–95
medicine 11, 43, 44–45, 56, 61, 117
Microsoft Xbox 39
Mimica Touch 98–99
Minecraft 38–39
mosquitos 40–41

nanotechnology 58–59

ocean 11, 70, 71, 73, 81, 86–87, 88–89
organs 49, 52–53, 57

Pakštaitė, Solveiga 99
Paralympics 78–79
passports 12–13
phones 26, 30–31, 33, 36, 37, 45, 59, 90, 97, 106, 122–23
photographs 15, 25, 29, 35
Piantanida, Nick 77
Piccard, Jacques 71

planes 6–7, 11, 14, 63, 66–67, 76, 85, 112–13, 123
plastic 42, 82–83, 88–89, 114, 125
pollution 25, 82–83, 88, 100–1, 104, 105, 115
prosthetics 124–25

quadstick 39

rescue 4–5, 10–11
Robertson, Seth 85
robots 10–11, 18, 19, 74–75, 80, 92–93, 109, 118–19, 124–25
Rochester Cloak 121
Rubik's Cube 74–75

Safari Seat 17
security 12–13, 14–15, 75
smartphones 31, 33, 37, 90, 97, 106
Smog Tower 100–1
social media 35
solar power 72, 91, 105
soldiers 19, 51
space 11, 24, 42, 66, 67, 68–69, 70, 76–77, 85, 109, 110–11
SpecialEffect 38
sports 59, 74, 78–79, 106–7
stealth plane 6–7
stem cells 42, 95
Stratolaunch 66–67
surgery 43, 46–47, 49, 61

Takats, Zoltan Dr. 47
tattoos 45, 50–51
ThrustSSC 62
Tito, Dennis 110
Tran, Viet 85
translation 36–37, 103
transport 8–9, 17, 29, 80–81, 95

Vacanti, Charles 43
video games 22–23, 38–39
virtual reality 23, 48–49
voice recognition 15, 32–33, 37, 39

Walsh, Don 71
waste 31, 82–83, 88, 89, 98–99, 105, 115
water 4, 31, 51, 63, 70, 71, 80, 81, 82, 83, 85, 86–87, 89, 90, 91, 123
wheelchairs 16–17
Williams, Serena 107
wind power 72–73, 91